D1187300

MASTER MANIPULATOR

HV
6770
T6
B75
1985

MASTER
MANIPULATOR

Homer Brickey, Jr.

amacom
AMERICAN MANAGEMENT ASSOCIATION

*This book is available at a special
discount when ordered in bulk quantities.
For information, contact Special Sales Department,
AMACOM, a division of American Management Association,
135 West 50th Street, New York, NY 10020.*

Library of Congress Cataloging-in-Publication Data

Brickey, Homer.
  Master manipulator.

  Includes index.
  1. Securities fraud—Ohio—Toledo—Case studies.
2. Brokers—Malpractice—Ohio—Toledo—Case studies.
3. White collar crime investigation —Ohio—Toledo—
Case studies. 4. Bell & Beckwith. I. Title.
HV6770.T6B75   1985   364.1'68'0977113   85-47675
ISBN 0-8144-5818-1

*© 1985 AMACOM, a division of
American Management Association, New York.
All rights reserved.
Printed in the United States of America.*

*This publication may not be reproduced,
stored in a retrieval system,
or transmitted in whole or in part,
in any form or by any means, electronic,
mechanical, photocopying, recording, or otherwise,
without the prior written permission of AMACOM,
a division of American Management Association,
135 West 50th Street, New York, NY 10020.*

Printing number

10 9 8 7 6 5 4 3 2 1

To
my three sons

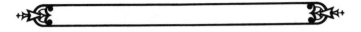

A Personal Introduction

February 7, 1983, started like many another Monday on the business beat. I got to work around 8:00, poured a cup of coffee from the honor-system pot, and began opening a considerable pile of weekend mail.

Someone handed me a memo from the Toledo *Blade*'s nightside staff saying the paper had received a tip that Bell & Beckwith, the city's oldest brokerage house, had been shut down by the regulatory authorities because of a shortage of millions of dollars. Any newspaper gets lots of rumors, mostly false, and there was no reason to think this one was true either. In fact, it was just plain incredible.

But our staff started to work on it, and by the end of the morning, we had the first in what was to be a long-running series of articles on the collapse of the brokerage firm. Even two years after the debacle, the story is still unfolding. And the aftereffects of the failure, which touched and changed the lives of many, still linger in the community.

Bell & Beckwith and two other brokerages that failed at about the same time—Stix & Co. in St. Louis and G. V. Lewellyn & Co. in Des Moines—have offered many lessons for regulators, other brokerages, and even investors. Three men who led amazingly similar lives were victims of their own overly ambitious dreams and proved that a system largely dependent on trust is vulnerable to gamblers who are daring enough to risk everything to achieve their goals.

The discovery that a man regarded as a philanthropist and an honest businessperson could steal millions showed me the truth of something an editor once told me: "There's very little difference between the best of us and the worst of us." I got caught up in the most fascinating story I have come across in over 20 years of newspapering. I hope the readers of the Bell & Beckwith story will also find it fascinating and useful.

Many thanks for inspiration, technical help, and information to several Toledo *Blade* staffers—Tom Gearhart, Pat Green, Tom Jewell, Randy Samborn, and Mary Reddington and her library crew—and to John Weglian, Joe Brainard, Bob and Ann Potter, Al Wagener, Barry Sucher, Mel Barger, Ed Esgain, and other Toledo-area people too numerous to mention. I appreciate Sue Cohan's thoughtful work in copy editing this book.

Thanks also to Judge Nicholas Walinski, liquidation trustee Pat McGraw, Ted Focht of the Securities Investor Protection Corp., and the staff of the Securities and Exchange Commission, especially Joyce (Lynch) Glynn, Ralph Buie, and William Goldsberry.

Much of Chapter 1 appeared originally in the Toledo *Blade* (and is used here by permission), and parts of several other chapters are based on information originally brought to light by the *Blade*. The excerpt from Edward Lamb's book *The Sharing Society* in Chapter 7 is used by permission of Lyle Stuart, Inc.

Contents

1

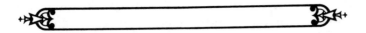

Just Another Examination

On a cold, blustery February day in 1983, Ralph Buie left his room at Toledo's Holiday Inn West, finished off his breakfast, and started driving his rented car toward downtown. An inch of snow left over from a savage winter storm the day before was still drifting over the city streets, making driving more of a chore than usual. But Buie, then an examiner with the Securities and Exchange Commission's Chicago office, had more on his mind than the weather. He had been in Toledo for 11 days, examining the records of the Bell & Beckwith brokerage, and if all went well, he would soon be on his way back to Chicago or off to examine another brokerage house. All wasn't going well, however, and that morning—February 4, 1983—Buie knew that by the end of the day, he might have to set in motion a procedure that would rock Toledo's financial community. And he knew that what he did could have a profound effect on the lives of the 46 Bell & Beckwith employees and their families.

But even Buie, who knew more about the case than anyone else at that point, was unaware of the full extent of what he had chanced upon. He had uncovered the largest stock-brokerage fraud in the SEC's history—$47 million worth. As a result of Buie's patient and persistent questioning and demands for greater documentation, a tangled web of deceit was uncovered that had withstood previous audits and examinations. The 85-year-old Bell & Beckwith brokerage was out of business, and a major industry of sorts— the bankruptcy of Bell & Beckwith—was created.

The Bell & Beckwith failure could be described as the case of 1,000 days and 7,000 nightmares. Although most of the 7,000 investors in the brokerage have become whole again, a handful still have not received all their money back. Some events happened that weekend in February 1983 with the speed of an avalanche; others are moving along more like a glacier. It took less than a day to convene a federal court hearing at a most unusual location, the motel on the grounds of Toledo Express Airport, and a dozen or so government and regulatory officials flew in from around the country that weekend, either to appear in the hastily convened court or to get firsthand information. By the next business day, Monday, February 7, Bell & Beckwith was suspended from the New York Stock Exchange. Exactly a week after Buie decided there was no backing out, the federal court declared Bell & Beckwith insolvent and appointed a bankruptcy trustee.

In contrast with the speed of the early proceedings, the settling of the firm's estate will take years. The trustee's $65 million suit against Bell & Beckwith's auditing firm, Frederick S. Todman & Co., for example, won't go to trial until three years after the collapse at the earliest. It took several months to reimburse the majority of the 7,000 investors. And it was a year and a half before the trustee proposed a partial distribution of money to 47 large investors who were over the insurance limits. Another 13—with accounts over $1.3 million each—are still owed a total of $2.4 million and will have to wait for a later distribution.

Buie also brought an end to the career of Bell & Beckwith's managing partner, Edward P. Wolfram, Jr., who is now serving a 25-year sentence in the Federal Correctional Institution in Tallahassee, Florida.

It now appears that the house of cards built by Ted Wolfram collapsed primarily because of a hotel-casino that was losing a horrendous amount of money—sometimes hundreds of thousands of dollars a month—and interest rates that rose rapidly in the early 1980s.

In the month that Bell & Beckwith failed, the prime interest rate hit its lowest point in four years, but the damage was already done. In the month before the collapse, the interest on Wolfram's $47 million debt to the firm totaled about $600,000. His alteration of documents to conceal the fraud was becoming more frenetic—and therefore more detectable.

So when Buie began his investigation that January, Bell & Beckwith was already a terminal case. But judging by the desperation of some of his cover-up maneuvers, Wolfram wasn't ready to admit it. And it appears that even if there were suspicions, no one in the firm knew how serious the trouble was.

Buie, now an enforcement attorney for the SEC in Atlanta, had no clue to the firm's financial deterioration or to Wolfram's fraud when he arrived in Toledo on January 24, 1983, for what he thought would be a routine examination of the records. He had a general feeling that Bell & Beckwith was a clean sort of operation. And why not? The genteel old firm had a reputation for catering to the carriage trade. And even though its venerable building on Erie Street was a bit shabby, the firm was planning a move to more modern offices in the restored Fort Industry Square historic district. Bell & Beckwith had the outward appearance of stability, solidity, and quiet wealth.

Buie says he never received a tip from anyone inside or outside the firm, but he did overhear a general comment from a New York Stock Exchange employee about a "concentration" problem in some of the firm's margin accounts. Too much of one stock was carried as collateral, and the SEC regulations say broadly, "You can't have all your eggs in one basket."

Wolfram supposedly had solved the concentration problem by putting additional collateral in a bank, and a telegram to that effect had been sent to the New York Stock Exchange. That telegram eventually played an important part in Buie's examination and was one of the red flags that made him skeptical and more inquisitive.

Through the examination, Buie steadily built up suspicion that something was amiss, but he also was aware that he *could* be wrong. No one signal by itself was conclusive. Each question raised had a logical answer. A bank confirmation statement didn't have a seal or stamp on it. Perhaps a clerk's error. Several columns of figures on a long statement didn't "extend" or "foot" properly (they didn't add correctly, either across or down). Again, a possible human error. A letter that should have been dated late 1982 carried a 1983 date. People in a hurry, especially during a holiday week, make mistakes.

But by the tenth day of examination—the Wednesday of Bell & Beckwith's last week in business—Buie knew that the future of the firm came down to its ability to prove the value of two large investments. If either one was worth anywhere near its stated value, the firm might suffer reprimands or some other form of punishment for rules infractions but would remain in business. If neither investment could produce the needed value, the firm would be closed down because it would be insolvent by at least $21 million (a figure revised upward several times since).

During the entire first week of the examination, Buie was concerned with seeing that Bell & Beckwith was in compliance with the net-capital rule, a very complicated regulation that basically requires a firm to have a sufficient financial safety cushion to withstand economic reversals. (A broker-dealer's total liabilities, for example, can't be more than 15 times its net capital, or net worth.) That part of the examination went routinely.

By the start of the second week of the examination, Buie was ready to turn his attention to an equally complicated regulation—the customer-protection rule—and he began a detailed analysis of the firm's margin accounts. A margin account allows a customer to buy securities by putting up half the money; or the customer can put up collateral valued at a certain amount and borrow up to 50 percent of that value from the brokerage. In Wolfram's case, his borrowings from Bell & Beckwith over a five-year period had totaled about $32 million, and accrued interest had boosted his total debt to $47 million. To secure the debt, he had two major assets in a number of margin accounts in a number of names—including that of his wife, Zula—and in several corporations.

Wolfram's accounts had for some time been secured mainly by a Japanese stock, Toto Ltd. (Toto is a manufacturer of plumbing fixtures, and its stock is traded on a number of exchanges around the world.) The stock was held in a custodial account at the New York brokerage of Drexel Burnham Lambert, to the point where 95 percent of his indebtedness was covered by that one stock. And his indebtedness (again, under a variety of names) accounted for more than 90 percent of the total margin debt of all the firm's customers.

It was that "concentration" that had caught the New York Stock Exchange's attention the previous fall. To correct the problem, Wolfram told exchange officials that he had put 95 issues of convertible bonds in an account at the First Interstate Bank of Nevada. Either piece of collateral would have been more than sufficient to support a debt of $47 million. The Toto stock carried a stated value of $278 million, and the bonds—according to a telegram received by the New York Stock Exchange—had a value of $105 million. So, on paper, Wolfram's borrowings totaled less than half of either piece of collateral.

Very quickly on the second week of the examination, things began to go wrong. Buie asked for the necessary documentation to support the margin debt of Wolfram's accounts and related accounts. Wolfram showed Buie a telegram that he said he had received from the Nevada bank to satisfy the New York Stock Exchange's query. Buie—a stocky, 51-year-old former Navy lieutenant and former broker with Francis I. DuPont—didn't take the telegram at face value. As a broker, he had had an earlier experience with a phony telegram, and he knew that a telegram could be sent by anyone, especially a telegram like the one Wolfram showed him. It bore a Las Vegas address but not the name of the bank.

So he asked for documentation of the securities count (quarterly box count) for December 31, 1982, and Wolfram produced a verification letter—actually a Bell & Beckwith letter sent to the Nevada bank requesting an accounting of the Wolfram bonds—returned with "verification" of the bonds' value. But Buie noticed that the letter had no bank stamp on it, and most such verification letters do. (Later, an even more glaring error showed up—the letter should have been dated December 31, 1982, but instead was dated December 31, 1983. People in a hurry do, indeed, make mistakes.)

Buie asked whose name the securities were registered in, and Wolfram replied that they were in Zula Wolfram's name. Buie called the SEC's Chicago office, and his supervisor, Michael O'Rourke, checked with several transfer agents for some of the different securities issues. There were 95 issues and numerous transfer agents. The Chicago office came up with no bonds in Zula Wolfram's name. When confronted with that information, Wolfram told Buie that the bonds probably had been transferred to a bank nominee's name, and he suggested that it could be Brown Co. or Brown & Co.

Buie got back to Chicago by telephone, and again O'Rourke checked with some transfer agents. By this time, Buie wanted hard evidence—he wanted to see the bonds. He told Wolfram, "I want your permission to go to Las Vegas to physically count them." Up to that time, Wolfram had been extremely congenial and pleasant, but his temperament began to change. He refused Buie's request, saying that it was an invasion of his wife's financial privacy and that the SEC had singled out her account for undue scrutiny because she was a wealthy woman and the wife of a partner.

So Buie told Wolfram he had no choice but to take the position that the bonds didn't exist and then go back to the original concentration problem—namely, the Toto stock at Drexel Burnham Lambert. If Wolfram could have privately borrowed perhaps $20 million or so, he could have paid down the margin debt enough to solve the problem, at least temporarily. Wolfram and a large Bell & Beckwith investor tried, without success, to raise that amount from Toledo Trust Co. (Toledo's largest bank) during Buie's examination.

By late Wednesday, the cat-and-mouse game was getting serious. Buie asked for a monthly statement of the stocks held for Bell & Beckwith by Drexel Burnham

Lambert. There was a delay. Wolfram said he couldn't find it. Buie was insistent. Some time later—Buie thinks it was Thursday—Wolfram produced a photocopy of the Drexel Burnham statement. Buie asked where the original was, and Wolfram said he couldn't find the folder. He said there was too much paperwork.

That was an important signal to Buie. If a brokerage can keep copies, why can't it keep originals?

In any case, the photocopy proved damaging enough. One set of figures loomed large, astronomically large, compared with others on the page, and when Buie tried to add them up on a calculator, they didn't total correctly—off by $8 million out of $278 million. And besides, the sheer size of the figure boggled the mind. Buie had been in the business long enough to know there are no publicly traded stocks valued at $96,000 a share. Wolfram had spread the word around the firm that his Toto shares were special—"founder's stock"—but the figure strained Buie's credulity.

Buie's heart sank. The evidence was in front of him, but he was hoping he wasn't right. There had to be a simple explanation. Besides, he wasn't *totally* sure. And he was struck by the sadness of realizing that a respected 85-year-old firm, a landmark in the community, could be on the verge of going out of business.

He immediately reported the discrepancy to Chicago. SEC officials in New York quickly got to Drexel Burnham and received a copy of the original statement.

About midday on Thursday, someone from the Chicago office called Buie at Bell & Beckwith and told him to go back to his motel room. What he was doing was too delicate to discuss on a line that could be overheard. Buie went to the Holiday Inn West and called back. Three or four people were in on the conference call. He began reading over the phone the information on the statement he had been given. He went through each item, each stock. The first one, Ajininomoto Co., was correct; the second one, CRA Ltd., was correct; the third one, Fuji Photo Film, was correct; and so on until he got down to Toto. At that point it was TILT—STOP. The original statement from Drexel Burnham plainly showed the 2,816 shares to be worth $1.80 each, or $5,068.80 in all.

In hindsight, the gross forgery now looks childishly simple. There were no overstrikes or erasures that would have caught instant attention. Through the simple addition of typewriter strokes, a figure of $1.80 a share became $96,141.80. And the $1.80 a share multiplied by 2,816 shares, or a total of $5,068.80, became $278,558,418.80. *But it didn't extend!* So simple. So crude. Yet so lucrative for so long.

But there was still one more slim possibility that Bell & Beckwith could be solvent—the $105 million in bonds, if it existed, would do it. Buie knew he had to make that final check.

Two SEC officials—Tom Huber, an attorney, and Larry Kendra, an examiner—flew to Las Vegas Thursday night, and on Friday morning they presented an SEC supoena to the First Interstate Bank. The bank had nothing to show. Wolfram had no securities there. (In fact, it turned out, the address Bell & Beckwith was mailing the verification statements to was Wolfram's own and not the bank's address.)

Things happened quickly from that point. Even as Buie was flying back to Chicago late that Friday to prepare an affidavit for court, Joyce Lynch, an attorney in the Chicago office, called Judge Nicholas Walinski, of the U.S. District Court in Toledo, at his home to arrange for a Saturday hearing on a temporary restraining order to shut the brokerage down. Judge Walinski said he would wait for a call on Saturday morning. Meanwhile, numerous other people were notified, and at least a dozen officials from Chicago, New York, and Washington packed their bags to head for Toledo overnight.

The Chicago contingent—including Buie, attorneys Huber and Lynch, and their boss, William Goldsberry, the regional administrator—arrived at Toledo Express Airport about 10:00 on Saturday morning. They called Judge Walinski, who said that, because the courthouse was closed, he would go to the airport and hold court there. By the time Judge Walinski arrived, one of the SEC staff had arranged for a conference room in the Airport Motel, a couple of hundred yards across the parking lot from the terminal.

Proceedings of the hearing were sealed until the following Monday, to protect the firm and the partners in case some way could be found to keep Bell & Beckwith open. Transcripts of that hearing have never been released by the court; the following account comes from the memory of several people who were present in the motel conference room.

Ted Wolfram showed up with his wife and his attorney, Frank McManus, after receiving a call that morning from Joyce Lynch. Two of the other seven general partners also arrived, as did two attorneys from Bell & Beckwith's law firm, Shumaker, Loop & Kendrick. Within an hour or so, several New York Stock Exchange officials, obviously eager for information and wanting to be near the source, arrived at the airport but were not directly a part of the conference-room court hearing.

Buie's sworn affidavit—hastily typed in the hectic hours before the hearing—was submitted to the judge, and Buie was called upon to answer several questions. When it became clear that a temporary receiver might be appointed, Joseph Shibley, a Toledo attorney, was summoned to the hearing. The judge signed the temporary restraining order, and Shibley started taking steps to secure the Bell & Beckwith building. Toward the end of the hearing—which went on until perhaps 1:30 in the afternoon—Wolfram left the courtroom. He put his hand on Ralph Buie's arm and remarked, "Don't worry; you did a good job."

By Monday, February 7, thanks to the rumor mill, many Toledoans knew something big was happening at Bell & Beckwith. Some even knew that the firm wouldn't open for business that morning, and there were rumors of shortages approaching $50 million (incredible as it seemed at the time, the figure turned out to be amazingly accurate). And, early on Monday, the New York Stock Exchange issued a terse message saying that Bell & Beckwith had been "summarily suspended as a member." Customers arriving at the brokerage that morning were met by a security guard hired by the temporary receiver, Shibley. The old place at 234 Erie Street was full of people, but they weren't Bell & Beckwith employees.

Events continued at a rapid pace. Ted and Zula Wolfram signed over all their property to Bell & Beckwith. And the Securities Investor Protection Corp., which insured the firm's deposits, announced that most of Bell & Beckwith's customers could expect to get their money back. On Thursday, February 10, Judge Walinski appointed Patrick McGraw, of the law firm of Fuller & Henry, as permanent trustee to settle the Bell & Beckwith estate. And on Friday, February 11, he declared before a packed courtroom that the firm was bankrupt.

Today, many months later, the case still makes news occasionally, and it grinds on. Lawsuits—some of which have been dropped and some of which continue—total in the hundreds of millions. The Securities Investor Protection Corp. has settled $39 million in investor claims (and raised its dues to member firms to accommodate the large payout and to restore its reserves to statutory levels). The Landmark Hotel and Casino in Las Vegas, once owned by Howard Hughes and later by the Wolframs—and the cause of the disappearance of at least $15 million of the diverted funds—has a new owner, William Morris. Under a complicated agreement involving $20 million or so for the highly mortgaged hotel, the Bell & Beckwith estate could net about $1.5 million if all goes well. Other Wolfram assets—a $2 million jet plane, two other planes, a Florida farm and stable of racehorses, a barnful of sports cars, oil and gas properties, two farms in Arkansas, and a house inspired by Frank Lloyd Wright along the Maumee River in the village of Grand Rapids, Ohio—have for the most part been disposed of.

For months, crews of accountants from Ernst & Whinney went to the old Bell & Beckwith building daily to continue the task of sorting out the paperwork mess. Legal fees are now beyond the $3 million mark, with a big suit for $65 million against the brokerage's last auditors, Frederick S. Todman & Co., still untried. The auditing firm has already been censured by the Securities and Exchange Commission and one of its partners suspended for six months. Two new brokerages sprang up in Toledo directly as a result of the Bell & Beckwith closing—Oberweis Securities, Inc. and Cowen & Co.—and they ended up hiring the majority of the failed brokerage's employees.

Officially, the SEC says that it sees no need for any regulatory changes, that the rules on the books are adequate. But the Bell & Beckwith case has left its mark on the industry. The level of consciousness of brokerage crime has been raised, the degree of skepticism heightened.

Ralph Buie, the examiner who cracked the Bell & Beckwith case, returned to his native South. He doesn't expect ever to see a similar fraud. "Fortunately for the industry, the Bell & Beckwith cases don't come along very often," he says. Buie has received a lot of pats on the back for his investigatory work in the matter. And he's working in a higher echelon now at a somewhat less hectic job. There are many twists of fate in the complex Bell & Beckwith case. Buie, for example, was born in Florida, not too many miles from where Wolfram will spend a large part of his life in prison. But the final twist of fate is that the man who broke the SEC's biggest brokerage-fraud case probably will never get a chance to work firsthand on anything like it in the future.

2

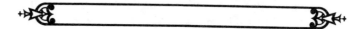

Seeds of Ambition

Ted Wolfram was a polyester man in a pinstripe world. He was more comfortable in a $1,000 pair of handcrafted snakeskin cowboy boots than in Gucci loafers. His idea of formal wear wasn't limited to a tuxedo—his wardrobe included $500 blue-jeans suits. A pickup truck shared his driveway with a BMW and a Mercedes. He could be seen in his $1,000-a-year seat at a Bowling Green State University football or basketball game in a business suit one time and a sombrero and boots another time. He liked Indian jewelry, initialed gold belt buckles, and paintings of wildlife and sporting events. His home displayed a wide range of art, from the tacky to the sublime—a cheap velvet painting of a horse, a Monet print, an unsigned painting of a football player, exquisite oils of waterfowl by Les Kouba.

Wolfram led at least two lives. As managing partner of Bell & Beckwith, he kept a low profile in Toledo business circles. But he had a far-flung business empire— and a $2 million Cessna jet and two propeller planes to keep him in touch with a racehorse farm in Florida, the Landmark Hotel and Casino in Las Vegas, farms in Arkansas, and an oil-exploration company in Baton Rouge, Louisiana.

His life-style was full of anomalies. Most of the Wolframs' properties were clearly rural. The farms in Arkansas and Missouri totaled about 3,000 acres in the rolling hills of the Ozarks, miles away from a city of any size. Their horse farm was in the countryside near Ocala, Florida. And their home, designed by a disciple of Frank Lloyd Wright, was built on a ravine cutting into the old Miami and Erie Canal and overlooking the Maumee River at Grand Rapids, Ohio, 25 miles outside Toledo. The house stands on ground that once served as a campsite for troops of Major General "Mad Anthony" Wayne on their way to fight the Indians at the famous Battle of Fallen Timbers in 1794. Today, the sleepy little river village of Grand Rapids looks almost the same as it did at the turn of the century.

And yet, when the Wolframs were in Las Vegas, where Zula ran a show-production company called Zula Productions, they lived in a $250,000 condominium in Regency Towers. And even as Bell & Beckwith was collapsing, they were planning to move into a 2,800-square-foot penthouse in Fort Industry Square, a block-long section of restored historic buildings in downtown Toledo overlooking the Maumee River. All in all, the Wolframs were not jet-setters, though. They had no social-club memberships and seldom took nonbusiness vacations.

Although his name, at least in the brokerage business, may eventually be as infamous as those of Vesco, Cornfeld, Sol Estes, and De Angelis, Ted Wolfram was an unlikely candidate for a $47 million scam. There's some evidence to suggest that he first illegally doctored records to prevent embarrassment and censure for an associate who came up short before an audit. And there's also some evidence that, except for a case of bad timing, he might have been able to dig his way out of the financial hole he fell into—and might have been able to cover his tracks in such a way that no one would ever have known what he did. Most people who knew him say he was one of the smartest men they ever met. And yet he made a monumental error of judgment in buying the Landmark Hotel just before the Las Vegas tourist business began a gradual—and for him, fatal—decline.

He had a chameleon personality. He could be arrogant as well as charming, a bully as well as an understanding friend. He cajoled, persuaded, frightened, sweet-talked, strong-armed, intimidated, and even bribed (with generous loans) his partners and employees into giving him a position of unchallenged power at the brokerage—an indiscretion for which they are all paying in a variety of ways.

Wolfram was a braggart and a supreme egotist. There wasn't anything he couldn't do, any contest he couldn't win, any challenge he couldn't beat. He was rough around the edges in some ways but fit in well in both worlds he inhabited. He could use the language of a sailor or barroom brawler at times and yet, in the words of an investor who lost hundreds of thousands of dollars, "he could charm the eyes out of a water buffalo." He purported to be an expert in history and horses, sports and gambling, and a variety of other things, including wines (he had 400 bottles in a cellar at home), food, jewelry, guns, and car racing. He seemed comfortable in a $1,000 business suit, wearing his gold Patek Philippe wristwatch and talking over a million-dollar business deal, and equally so wearing Levi's, chopping wood, and making small talk with a neighbor at his Grand Rapids home. (When Wolfram was mulling over a problem, he often chopped wood furiously as a form of release.) He was impatient, a fast talker and a fast thinker. A writer for Bowling Green's alumni magazine once wrote this about him: "He never uses 10 words when 50 will do. He delivers them in a racing-to-Apocalypse style that leaves the listener, but not Wolfram, out of breath. . . ." In the same interview, Wolfram commented: "I'm a fiercely competitive person. I don't even sit down to play checkers without expecting to win."

Ted Wolfram grew up in a typically conservative family in a typically conservative midwestern town, Maumee, Ohio, which is now a suburb of Toledo. When Edward Phillip Wolfram, Jr. was born, on September 8, 1930, Maumee was just a village, separated by miles and temperament from the wild and wicked Toledo of the Prohibition era.

He was the oldest of four sons of Edward and Mabel Wolfram. The Wolfram family had been a fixture in Maumee for years. Wolfram's father had gone to school there when Maumee could still be considered a horse-and-buggy town. The elder Wolfram—known as E.P.—went to St. Joseph's Catholic Church, and there began a series of events that led eventually to Ted Wolfram's rise to the top of Bell & Beckwith.

One of the pillars of the community back in the early 1920s was Grafton Mouen, Sr., managing partner of the relatively young Bell & Beckwith brokerage. Mouen (whose son Grafton, Jr. also was later to rise in the firm) attended St. Joseph's and took a liking to several young boys who went to the church and whose families he knew well. Over a period of several years, he hired all of them at Bell & Beckwith—Ed Wolfram, Ed Esgain, Raymond Servais, Joseph Pfleghaar, and Clarence Brell. Ed Wolfram was one of the first to be hired, in 1920, a year before the firm changed its name from Secor & Bell to Bell & Beckwith. In the early 1920s, cars were scarce in Maumee, so it was natural for the five contemporaries to share one. They bought an old Ford and took turns driving the ten miles or so to the brokerage in downtown Toledo.

The firm had a civilized touch about it. It bought

bushels of apples, peaches, and oranges to deliver to customers. The women who changed the quotations on the firm's big board handed out boxes of Cracker Jacks for customers to munch on while listening to the World Series on the radio. Although Mouen was something of an autocrat, the firm operated as one big family. Even during the depression, Bell & Beckwith's carriage trade stuck by the brokerage, and on the rare occasions when a customer couldn't make a margin call, the partners kicked in the money. During the depression the firm had to cut wages, but it didn't let any of its staff go.

Although Ed Wolfram eventually became a general partner in Bell & Beckwith, it was a long pull. Through the depression he was lucky to make $65 a month, hardly enough to raise a family in middle-class fashion. The Wolframs eventually showed a few signs of prosperity (like a summer cottage at Devil's Lake in Michigan), but they never lived appreciably better than their less affluent neighbors. In fact, the Wolfram family rented a house for many years before finally building a home after Ted was out of high school.

Ted Wolfram was very much like his father in some ways—aggressive, clever, and charming, but sometimes aloof and capable of displaying an explosive temper. Although the extended family was not particularly close-knit, Ted's wing of the family was. And in the late 1960s, he built a home in Grand Rapids next to his father's less pretentious house there. Ted had aunts, uncles, and cousins in Maumee but saw them less and less frequently as years went on. He seemed uncomfortable around his relatives. (In later years, he fired his brother Paul from a management job at the hotel-casino.)

Ted was the most aggressive and, ostensibly, the smartest of the boys. At St. Joseph's (where he was an altar boy), at Maumee High School, and later at Bowling Green

State University, he could name his grade. He could get an *A* in any class that he considered worthy of his effort. But he never worked fewer than 30 hours a week, even in high school, and by the time he was in college, he had other interests, too. His final grade point average at Bowling Green was 2.65 out of a 4.0 total—in other words, a *B*-minus or *C*-plus average—even though his IQ of 126 demonstrated superior intelligence.

The 1948 Maumee High yearbook, *The Reflector,* showed a skinny Ted Wolfram with the caption: "Wavy hair—never at a loss for words." That part always remained true. He was a talker, and the faster he talked, the closer he got to stuttering. He had an opinion or an answer for everything. The skinny, 5-foot 10-inch kid gave way to a not-so-skinny man over the years—and at times, to shed the pounds, Wolfram resorted to fasting.

He was in the boys' glee club for two years, on the track team for a year (he ran the 110-yard high hurdles and the 220-yard low hurdles), in the choir for four years, in the Hi Y club for two years, and appropriately, in dramatics for two years. He tried out for the football team but never became a starter. He was the senior class president, and the yearbook showed him at the top of an oval picture of the class officers underneath the caption: "Sitting on Top of the World."

One of Wolfram's closest friends in high school was Roscoe Betz, also one of the 71 graduating seniors in 1948. Betz (known then as "Sonny" and now known as Ross) was born on the same day as Ted. He lived with the Wolfram family for a time and went to Maumee High School after his parents moved away.

Ted Wolfram, the son of a broker; Sonny Betz, the son of an A&P executive; and Al Wagener, the son of a factory production manager—all were the closest of friends, the "Three Musketeers." The three would shoot crows at night along the Maumee River (for a bounty), sometimes firing off 300 or 400 shotgun rounds a night. They were constant companions even after high school. In 1950 they made a pact to join the Air Force together, since war in the Far East seemed a likely—exciting—possibility. But by the end of 1950, only Al Wagener was in the Air Force. Sonny Betz had stayed at Miami University (of Ohio), and Ted Wolfram enrolled at Bowling Green State University, about 10 miles from Maumee, where he joined the Delta Upsilon fraternity. Before going to Bowling Green, Wolfram had attended Xavier University in Cincinnati briefly but quit when he couldn't find a good part-time job. He was also unhappy about the absence of female students. Even though they split up, Wolfram, Betz, and Wagener remained good friends—at least until February 1983. Betz was a general partner in Bell & Beckwith at the time of its collapse, and he was the first of the firm's partners to declare bankruptcy after the failure. Wagener is a crew leader for The Andersons (an agribusiness complex), supervising the unloading of farm chemicals from Great Lakes ships.

Wolfram was one of the few students to have his own transportation in Maumee High School in those days. He drove a 1936 Ford V-8. And although he dated a few of the Maumee girls, he mostly hung out with the guys at the Koral Hamburg, a short-order joint that served as a teenagers' gathering place. He worked for a while as a mechanic and jack-of-all-trades at Boellner's Sohio station. To earn money for college, he worked at the Toledo Plate & Window Glass Co. making ground-glass refrigerator trays, and he held construction jobs over several summers. He sold cars for a time and also repaired radios in his basement as a sideline. Things came easily to him, and he worked hard at getting along with everybody. He was regarded as something of a deal maker, a hotshot, and, by some, a smart aleck.

He especially liked to hang around the jocks, and he announced football games for Maumee High. Even though Wolfram was regarded as one of the "brains," most of his friends were football or basketball players. (One of his classmates, though not a close friend, was Dick Kazmaier, who went on to become a Heisman trophy winner on the Princeton football team.) Years later, Wolfram displayed his love for sports by becoming the biggest "sugar daddy" for Bowling Green State University's athletic program, donating more than $25,000 over a period of several years, in addition to throwing parties and dinners for athletic boosters and the teams. He befriended coaches and players alike and once gave a hotel job to a seven-foot basketball player he was wooing for Bowling Green (the player rewarded Wolfram's generosity by deciding to play for a Nevada team). And for a time he turned over a large old house in Grand Rapids to Mark Miller, a highly touted quarterback at Bowling Green who was trying to build a professional career. Wolfram also gave him a summer job as a trainee at Bell & Beckwith. A charter member of Bowling Green's Falcon Club (an athletic booster organization), Wolfram was active in the university's alumni association investment committee as well and once was honored by the school during a football halftime.

When football coach Don Nehlen was fired by Bowling Green, Wolfram was so irate that he called members of the university's board of directors to complain. (Nehlen, who went on to coach under Bo Schembechler at the University of Michigan and later became head coach at West Virginia, testified as a character witness for Wolfram at Wolfram's sentencing.)

Wolfram wanted so badly to be named to Bowling

Green's board that he contributed nearly a quarter of a million dollars to political campaigns just months before the collapse of Bell & Beckwith—in hopes of getting a board appointment in return. In the primary campaign before the 1982 general election, he went to a fund raiser held by Jerry Springer, a Cincinnati councilman and former mayor who had aspirations of being the Democratic candidate for governor of Ohio. Wolfram pressed into the hands of a surprised Springer a check for $170,000. But Springer's campaign faltered, possibly because of the discovery that he had paid a prostitute by check at a Kentucky health spa. He lost out in the primary to another Democrat, Richard Celeste, who was elected governor that November. To hedge his bet, Wolfram gave a $50,000 check to the Celeste campaign. In fact, Wolfram, a registered Democrat who didn't mind saying he had voted for Richard Nixon, almost had a part-time political career himself. He once considered running for state representative but backed out when he realized the time commitment that a campaign would involve.

After graduating with a business administration degree (finance major) from Bowling Green in 1953, Wolfram got an ROTC commission as a lieutenant in the Air Force and learned to fly fighter jets. He was sent as a finance officer to Atterbury Air Force Base (later renamed Bakalar Air Force Base) in Columbus, Indiana, where he met Zula VanScyoc, an 18-year-old laboratory worker at Bartholomew County Hospital. Zula, daughter of a civil service worker at Fort Benjamin Harrison, was one of the queen's attendants at a sports-car rally sponsored by the Air Force base and the local Jaycees group. Wolfram was one of the officers of the event, held on the runways of the air base.

When Ted Wolfram and Zula VanScyoc first met, it wasn't exactly love at first sight. Although Zula was an unsophisticated young woman, she was not totally impressed by the glib and cocky lieutenant. Nevertheless, they saw more and more of each other, and they were married on September 11, 1954, in Shelbyville, Indiana. The couple shared a great many interests—money, jewelry, travel, horses, Las Vegas. But there were some differences, too. Zula Wolfram always seemed genuinely at ease with whatever crowd she entered. She loved parties and company. And she would do almost anything to be a good sport—even to the point of smoking a cigar and telling jokes with the "boys" and going duck hunting with Ted and his friends. Ted also liked parties, but only to a point, and he sometimes tired of the company and withdrew from the conversation. He seldom drank much, and when he was fasting for weight control, he didn't drink at all.

Wolfram showered gifts, money, and affection on Zula. Almost everything they owned was in Zula's name, including the businesses and most of the margin accounts that served as the conduit for his diversion of funds from the brokerage. A partial list of the personal items signed over to the bankruptcy court after the collapse of Bell & Beckwith included rings, necklaces, and pendants valued for quick sale (about 50 percent less than wholesale value) at $45,000, along with a natural cerulean and white mink jacket valued at $2,800, a natural fitch coat with red fox tuxedo front appraised at $3,500, and half a dozen other furs.

Wolfram's generosity to his wife came slowly at first. Shortly after they were married and Wolfram began work for Bell & Beckwith as a salesman (after being a trainee at Hayden Stone in New York), he had to borrow $7,500 from Zula's former employer to make the down payment on their first house. It took several years to pay the loan back to the pathologist in Columbus.

But the brokerage business went well in the 1960s and 1970s, and Wolfram started to show signs of affluence.

It isn't certain when simple affluence turned into extravagance. It could have begun as early as 1968, when he began building a massive stone and wood house on the banks of the Maumee River next to a sandstone house his parents had built there. He wanted to be near his parents to help them in their old age. (Ironically, the homes of both Wolframs, father and son, were built largely of stone quarried at Whitehouse, Ohio, at the Toledo House of Corrections, a facility that incarcerated thousands of lawbreakers over the years.) Ted's house, valued after the Bell & Beckwith collapse at $309,000, resembled a hunting lodge. Typical of Frank Lloyd Wright derivatives, it was set into the hillside, and much of the furniture was built in. Wolfram had made much of the furniture and cabinets himself. "Our house is an extension of nature," Wolfram once told the Bowling Green alumni magazine. "I can walk into our living room in my hip boots after duck hunting and then change into a tuxedo for a party an hour later. It lends itself to both."

First-time visitors to the Wolfram home were sometimes astonished to see peacocks roaming the lawn in the warm months. The birds were a gift from Joseph Schedel, a wealthy customer of Wolfram's who collected jade, bronzes, and exotic wildlife. The Wolfram's also had caged snakes in their home.

It was appropriate that Ted and Zula met at a race, since racing has been an important theme in their lives ever since. They raised championship-quality standardbred horses and have owned many sports cars. They entertained friends and associates at Indianapolis 500 races (sometimes buying as many as 40 seats a year). And Wolfram once tried to get together a deal to buy the Indianapolis 500 racetrack. He also toyed with the idea of building a race-car factory in Toledo, across the alleyway from the Bell & Beckwith brokerage.

Wolfram was attracted to racing at an early age. As a teenager, he built and raced go-carts, and he sold programs at the horse races at the Lucas County fairgrounds. Although Wolfram was out of high school before he got his first sports car, he bought many later. At the time of the collapse of Bell & Beckwith, he owned so many sports and racing cars that they had to be housed in a barn some distance from his home. He had spent over $70,000 in one year to sponsor race cars and equipment for two racing outfits. His stable of cars included eight relatively rare OSCAs (Officina Specializzata Costruzione Automobili), made in Bologna, Italy, plus a 1967 Lamborghini, a 1964 Maserati, a 1971 Mercedes, a 1979 Mercedes, a 1977 BMW, and five other personal cars.

The Wolframs enjoyed some success at horse racing. Their 155-acre horse farm, Country Boy Estates, near Ocala, Florida—owned jointly with Carl and Mae Jean Allen (Allen is a former standardbred driver)—raised as many as 90 pacers and trotters with a possible sale value in the millions.

One of the Country Boy horses, Mo Bandy, won the Yonkers Open Trot in 1981 as a three-year-old. The colt won almost $100,000 in that race, the first leg of the famed Triple Crown of trotting. Another Wolfram horse, Zula Bird, was the two-year-old filly pacer of the year in Ohio in 1980. And another ridden by Allen, a former Detroit vacuum-cleaner distributor and professional motorcycle racer, won an $875,000 purse. All together, the Wolframs put about $6 million into their horse farm in five years.

Wolfram was generous with the money that he diverted from Bell & Beckwith and its customers' accounts. Just before Christmas 1982, the Salvation Army in Toledo was having a rough time collecting enough money to fill Christmas baskets for the thousands of needy people whose lot had been worsened by the deep recession.

25

Wolfram came forward and anonymously donated $25,000 to the Christmas fund on top of the $35,000 he had donated earlier in the year.

That same Christmas, he held a party for Bell & Beckwith employees and spouses at Belmont Country Club outside Toledo. The event featured a lavish spread of hors d'oeuvres, smoked salmon, and champagne and an open bar for the 50 guests. On some Christmases, Wolfram surprised employees with gifts from his own pocket rather than from the firm. One year, he gave every employee a watch, and half a dozen of the key women employees got $500 in cash from Wolfram.

He frequently treated employees, business associates, and friends to free lodging at the Landmark Hotel and Casino in Las Vegas, and sometimes he flew them out in his plane, often piloted by Paul Goldsmith, a former Indianapolis race-car driver.

Both Ted and Zula Wolfram made numerous loans to employees, friends, and, it appears, even some casual acquaintances. The loans, totaling nearly half a million dollars, included one for $200,000 to a group of business-people (among them a Bell & Beckwith broker) who were seeking to form a new company, Liberty Airlines, and take it public through a stock offering. Lovelace Watkins, a Las Vegas entertainer who worked for a time at the Landmark, got a total of 13 loans for more than $130,000. But many of the Wolfram loans were for relatively small amounts—$24,000 to a gas-station owner in Grand Rapids, $6,000 to another Las Vegas entertainer, $41,500 to a would-be race-car driver, and many smaller loans (including $5,500 to Don Nehlen, the former football coach at Bowling Green whose firing had so angered Wolfram).

Among the many loans he made to Bell & Beckwith employees were $260,000 to his high school buddy (and partner) Roscoe Betz, $100,000 to John Ayling (another broker), more than $30,000 to partner Thom McGhee, and more than $10,000 to Donald Henninger to help him buy in as a partner in the firm. He also lent a disputed amount to Robert Fox, one of the firm's brokers and a former partner, who started a business that ultimately failed. (The liquidation trustee claimed Fox owed Wolfram $143,000; Fox claimed the figure was between $70,000 and $80,000. The amount was finally fixed by the court as $132,000.)

Those who knew Wolfram—especially those who knew his family in his growing-up years—might have good reason to wonder how a man who made his own furniture and who once repaired radios for a few dollars could go through $32 million ($47 million with interest) in five years. Then again, Ted Wolfram was quoted in the Bowling Green alumni magazine a decade before the collapse of Bell & Beckwith as saying: "We were a tough bunch of kids. We used to joke that the odds were five to one that we'd all end up in jail eventually."

3

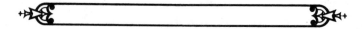

Wolfram the Manipulator

Ted Wolfram had a fire inside him, an ambition that would lie smoldering until a new idea fanned it into flames. It was this ambition that drove him to become managing partner of Bell & Beckwith and that compelled him to enter into one risky venture after another. And it was this ambition that finally consumed him. The debt became ever larger, and the options for discharging the debt became fewer.

Wolfram had a scheme a minute, it seemed. He had plans to make the Landmark Hotel and Casino the biggest and best development in Las Vegas. He was going to have the most successful stable in harness racing. He was going to build the fastest Indy car. He was going to turn a placid Arkansas farm into a fancy lake-country resort with a golf course designed by Jack Nicklaus. He was going to strike oil and gas in the Southwest. He was going to pull off a stock-market coup and take over profitable little companies when their stock hit a low point. And, perhaps more than anything else, he was going to make his wife proud of his achievements.

Wolfram was on the way to fulfilling some of these

schemes when things began to go wrong. However good his business instincts may have been, they were overshadowed by bad timing. In particular, the Landmark Hotel, which seemed like a steal in 1978, lost $15 million in less than five years, all of which flowed through Bell & Beckwith's cash and margin accounts.

How Wolfram got into a position to engineer his acquisitions—and eventually his and Bell & Beckwith's demise—is a case study in the accumulation of power. Essentially, he moved into a power vacuum, played on the weaknesses of his partners and the greed of some of his customers (in the later stages of Wolfram's cash-flow problem, Bell & Beckwith was offering more than 10 percent interest on cash deposits at a time when the money market called for 9 percent or less), and consolidated his power by making full use of his forceful personality.

By the end, Wolfram's ability to steal $47 million from the firm hinged on his having control of three critical functions: He was the managing partner, the partner in charge of compliance, and the partner in charge of margin accounts. Whatever checks and balances may have been intended for the firm disappeared under that arrangement. He was rubber-stamping his own fraud.

Actually, Wolfram had begun diverting money and securities long before. His manipulation of financial records began as early as 1973, and he didn't become managing partner until 1978.

The classic embezzlement has three elements— opportunity, motive, and justification. The opportunity for Wolfram to steal at first came accidentally, in the early 1970s, when his duties included pricing securities held for collateral in margin accounts. A monthly statement detailing foreign stocks held for Bell & Beckwith customers at a New York brokerage contained an error—through a typographical or clerical mistake, the price of a stock was

29

inflated. The mistake went uncorrected for some time, and Wolfram discovered two things: that the figures could be manipulated and that probably no one would know the difference.

The motive for committing his first fraud also developed accidentally. The firm was facing an audit, and Wolfram discovered that a partner, George Todd, had a serious deficiency in one of his accounts. Fearing that he and Todd and the firm itself might suffer censure or worse, Wolfram placed enough collateral in the Todd account—collateral that later turned out to be phony—to satisfy the auditors. At times in the late 1970s, Todd's accounts were as much as $500,000 in the red, and at the time of Bell & Beckwith's collapse in early 1983, one of his accounts had a debit of $400,000 and even with offsetting securities had a negative net worth of $258,887. Todd, the oldest of the partners at the time of the firm's collapse, stayed beyond his seventieth birthday. He was a kindly gentleman, a member of the firm for 47 years and a partner since 1946. Todd became the signator for the New York Stock Exchange seat in 1949. Todd hated to see young sales reps fail and, on occasion, would invent things for them to do to make a few dollars during their tryout period. A number of times he sent trainees to places like the Detroit airport to pick up employees or family members and rewarded them with $100 or $200 for their effort.

Later, the motivation for perpetuating and enlarging the fraud was Wolfram's own financial gain. In 1978 he engineered the purchase of the Landmark Hotel and Casino by putting a $1 million Bell & Beckwith Treasury security in Toledo Trust Co. under his wife's name and then using that as collateral for a $1 million letter of credit at a Las Vegas bank. The letter of credit, combined with a $1 million loan and a $250,000 wire transfer to Las Vegas, served as the down payment on the $12.5 million deal.

And toward the end of Bell & Beckwith, the need to take even larger amounts of money grew for several reasons—the hotel was losing $300,000 to $400,000 a month, and interest rates galloped in the late 1970s and early 1980s to the point where interest charges to the various Wolfram margin accounts approached $600,000 a month. After the hotel's perennial money-losing situation was apparent, Wolfram began diverting funds to buy other businesses that he thought could generate quick profits to extricate himself from the worsening financial mess he was in.

At first the justification for his fraud was simply to save Todd, the firm, and himself from embarrassment and censure, but later the justification became the economic survival of Bell & Beckwith and himself. The level of desperation is evident in the figures. Over 90 percent of the firm's margin debt was concealed in more than a dozen Wolfram-related accounts (under a variety of names, but all for his benefit), and Wolfram's $47 million indebtedness used up the lion's share of the firm's $54 million in customer deposits.

Rising interest rates produced a double whammy. The $600,000 or so in monthly interest charges demanded ever greater escalation of collateral, and it forced the firm to raise greater and greater amounts of cash from its customers. Compounding the problem was Wolfram's obsession with creating new businesses. His cash withdrawals (from a variety of accounts) in the final year of Bell & Beckwith's existence totaled $10.4 million, and he diverted $722,000 worth of securities in the same period.

Two of Bell & Beckwith's top producers, Robert Fox in Toledo and branch salesman Barry Sucher in Defiance, Ohio, had customers who accounted for an inordinate share of the $54 million in cash deposits. (Fox's customers alone had more than $6 million deposited, ostensibly for stock-trading purposes, but many of the customers were simply taking advantage of the firm's interest rates, which were higher than those of competitors.) If either broker had left Bell & Beckwith and taken a substantial portion of his business with him, the firm and Wolfram's career might have collapsed far earlier. And if market forces had made the stock market vastly preferable to the money market—causing customers to start using their free credit balances to buy stock—the firm would have been in grave jeopardy. Any serious diminution of cash balances would have caused problems for Wolfram.

Wolfram was very successful with auditors, at least partly because he disarmed them with his seeming integrity and frankness. For one thing, he was careful to surround himself with honest employees. (Given the nature of his own fraud, that was understandable—he couldn't risk, as one investigator put it, a problem within a problem.) And he never even so much as offered to go to lunch with an auditor—after all, the appearance of evil can be just as damaging as the actual fact of wrongdoing. During some of the early audits, Wolfram showed the most damning evidence—the margin accounts holding the inflated Toto stock—first, and voluntarily. Then he carefully explained the pricing of the stock and the reasons for its unusually high value, and the auditors went on to other matters. And why not? What thief is going to show the evidence before the investigation starts? And every audit that passed with flying colors strengthened the illusion that nothing was improper.

Wolfram had several devices for throwing his partners and fellow employees off guard. He occasionally manipulated the figures downward as well as upward—to give the impression that the stock price was reacting realistically to market forces. And his fictitious collateral wasn't just barely enough to cover the margin debt (a maneuver that might have aroused suspicion); rather, it was far in excess of the amount needed. His "collateral" totaled $383 million, while less than $100 million would have been sufficient.

Wolfram's fraud was made easier because of four bits of fiction that were perpetuated around the firm: that he had invested early in Japanese companies (like Toto) and had received "founder's stock," vastly more valuable than regular shares; that he had inherited a great deal of money from a wealthy industrialist, Joseph Schedel; that Zula Wolfram had inherited a fortune; and that the Landmark Hotel and Casino was doing very well (the truth of the matter was that the Landmark alone destroyed nearly half the $32 million Wolfram diverted over a five-year period).

Everyone in the partnership had responsibilities, but the partners were more interested in selling than in administration. Wolfram's strength seemingly was in administration—he majored in finance in college, served as a finance officer in the Air Force, and clearly was the most aggressive of the partners at the staid Bell & Beckwith firm.

He surrounded himself with partners who were willing to let him absorb the power. Besides Todd, a 15 percent partner, and Betz, a 13.5 percent partner like Wolfram, each of the others—J. Robert Jesionowski, Robert Coon II, Thom McGhee, John Thompson, and Donald Henninger—owned 8 percent or less of the company. (Thirty-four percent of the firm was owned by the partnership as a whole.) Some of this motley crew married money, some inherited it, some borrowed it to get into the firm. Besides Wolfram, there was another second-generation partner at the time of the brokerage collapse: Robert Coon II followed his father, who died of heat exhaustion in his car in front of the brokerage in 1964.

One of the partners, John Thompson, had left the

Toledo branch of Merrill Lynch to buy into Bell & Beck-with. Thompson ended up suffering in several ways. Not only did he incur the same general liability as the other partners—the liability for the Wolfram fraud—but his family's huge cash deposits were tied up for many months and are still not totally settled. Thompson had married into Toledo's wealthy and prestigious Jones family, and his two sons, John, Jr. and James, and daughter, Julie Berlacher, each had more than $400,000 on deposit at the time of collapse. The Securities Investor Protection Corp. insures each depositor for up to $100,000 in cash. Each of Thompson's children is still owed between $54,000 and $60,000 after the first distribution of funds in the Bell & Beckwith bankruptcy.

In any case, in the absence of a stronger force, Wolfram manipulated himself into a position of power, he manipulated the records to create false collateral, and he manipulated the auditors and examiners—at least until Ralph Buie's examination. The examination that finally caught Wolfram took place nearly ten months after the previous audit (conducted in April 1982), and fully a third of his diversion of funds took place in the firm's final year of business, mostly since its last audit.

Although Wolfram completely dominated Bell & Beckwith in its last three or four years, it wasn't always that way. As a young broker in the mid-1950s, he was ambitious, even brash at times, but hardly domineering. He was learning the brokerage business and waiting for a chance to exercise his political skills.

One of Wolfram's early customers, Joseph Schedel, who started doing business with the firm in 1958, instilled an even greater ambition in Wolfram and unknowingly gave him some of the credibility and leverage he needed to divert millions from the firm in later years. Schedel also gave Wolfram a taste of money and a taste for luxury.

Wolfram saw firsthand at Schedel's country estate in Elmore, Ohio, the accoutrements of wealth that could accrue even to a relatively poor immigrant.

Schedel, a German engineering graduate, came to northwestern Ohio in 1931 and lived in a $20-a-month apartment over a store while he worked on a process for manufacturing dolomite, a material used in making steel. He perfected the process, and for years his company—Dolite, in Gibsonburg, Ohio—was the only U.S. manufacturer of refractory dolomite. (He later sold the firm to Charles Pfizer & Co.) Schedel was a collector of rare and expensive jade and Chinese bronzes, and he was the author of a book, *The Splendor of Jade*. He also raised prizewinning Angus cattle and exotic waterfowl from all over the world. He traveled widely to collect unusual plants and animals for his baronial estate—a veritable wildlife preserve and arboretum with a Japanese garden surrounded by 350 varieties of trees.

As with so many events in Wolfram's life, his meeting Schedel was pure chance. Schedel had large amounts of money to invest by the late 1950s and was shopping around for a trustworthy broker. He first tried some of the larger New York firms, but, as a test, he didn't tell any of the brokers he was wealthy—rather, he offered to buy only a 100-share block of a cheap stock. He wasn't happy with the way he was treated, and when he visited Bell & Beckwith, Wolfram greeted him warmly and handled his small trade. Schedel, who never lost his thick German accent, was especially pleased that Wolfram was of German descent. (The name *Wolfram* comes from *Wolfhraben*, a centuries-old German surname derived from "wolf" and "raven," the companions of the chief god Wotan in Teutonic mythology.)

Within a few weeks, Schedel visited Bell & Beckwith again and bought additional stock from Wolfram. He liked Wolfram's style, and Wolfram came to admire Schedel's ambition and success. Their business relationship, which grew as Schedel gained confidence in Wolfram, developed into a friendship as well. At times Schedel put as much as $6 million into Bell & Beckwith, and he frequently called Wolfram on almost a daily basis. Schedel's business was a boost to Wolfram's career. And when Wolfram began his own entrepreneurship by buying first the hotel and later other properties, Wolfram's deals were plausible to Bell & Beckwith partners and employees because of the knowledge that Schedel was capable of backing ambitious projects.

Ironically, Schedel's investments at Bell & Beckwith, while providing a boost early in Wolfram's career, proved to be a detriment later on. When Schedel died in 1981, his estate moved a large amount of money out of the firm at a time when Wolfram was making ever larger cash infusions into the Landmark Hotel and Casino to keep it afloat. At the time of Bell & Beckwith's collapse, the Schedel estate had only slightly over $1 million in the firm, of which nearly $410,000 was in cash.

Wolfram also had credibility because of his real estate ventures. He was chairman of the board of Real Estate Concepts, Inc., a conglomeration of Toledo and Florida businesspeople with some ambitious plans. The group did develop a part of what is now Brandywine Country Club near Toledo. And it announced grand plans for a ski resort in Colorado (with 2,000 planned condominium units), a swim and tennis club at Sanibel Island, Florida, and a development at Lake Tahoe, Nevada, before quietly disbanding.

Wolfram's rise in Bell & Beckwith resulted from a number of events, some of them happenstance and some by design. The fact that his father had been with the firm for many years and had risen to become a general partner himself helped, as did the death of Grafton Mouen, the managing partner who had been a power in the firm through the boom years of the 1920s and the meager years of the depression before becoming senior partner in 1938. He ruled the firm through most of the 1960s. Under Mouen's leadership, Bell & Beckwith prospered, acquired a prestigious client list, and gained a reputation for solidity.

It was also Mouen who brought Wolfram's father, E.P., and many another young future partner into the firm. By the time of his death in 1967, Mouen owned 40 percent of Bell & Beckwith, and his death opened the way for the entry of several additional partners, one of whom was Ted Wolfram. A new partnership agreement was drawn up to limit partners to a maximum of 13.5 percent ownership, with the exception of George Todd, who was "grand-fathered" at 15 percent. Wolfram and Roscoe Betz, his friend since high school, came in at the maximum 13.5 percent.

The inexperience of some of the new partners was a point in favor of Wolfram's leadership, as was his obvious ambition and his background in finance. But he might never have become managing partner except for another chance event, which happened in 1976. Grafton Mouen's son, also named Grafton and a general partner in the firm, was suspended by the Securities and Exchange Commission for 20 days for giving inside information about Pelorex Corp. to customers and inducing customers to buy the stock at inflated prices. The SEC censured Bell & Beckwith because of the incident, and the partners used that as an excuse to squeeze Mouen out of the firm.

Mouen's departure further solidified Wolfram's claim to leadership, and after lobbying for it, he got the managing partner's job in 1978. By that time, he was, as noted, also the partner in charge of compliance and the partner in charge of margin accounts.

He had a talent for intellectually browbeating his associates, and occasional opposition to his plans was met with a barrage of information—and, sometimes, with temper. Wolfram's various margin accounts were well obfuscated by a variety of names that wouldn't automatically connect them to him. And on occasion, when a partner was asked to approve a large check that obviously was going to one or another of Wolfram's enterprises, he might shrug his shoulders, but he always signed. Wolfram demanded such scrupulous honesty of others that no one would have dared question his own integrity.

In effect, Wolfram bought loyalty by his generosity with employees. On a number of occasions, he lent large sums of money to employees who were having financial or personal problems (he lent one female employee enough money to buy a mobile home).

And he used a number of ploys to manipulate the considerable paperwork through the firm's maze. He told one clerk, for example, to double-check every stock price, but there were a few, he said, that he would be in a better position to check on, since he was in daily communication with the firm holding the stocks (one of which was, of course, the Toto stock that was greatly overvalued on Bell & Beckwith's books).

Another clerk was supposed to send quarterly letters to a bank in Las Vegas to verify a list of bonds carried on the books at $105 million. Had she sent the first letter to the bank, the nonexistence of the bonds would have been immediately clear. However, Wolfram used a clever ploy to divert that letter. He simply removed it from the out basket when the woman left for lunch. On his next trip to Las Vegas, he called her at Bell & Beckwith and told her that the bank never received the verification letter. He asked her what address it was sent to, and when she replied (with the bank's correct address), he told her the bank had changed to a lock box. He gave her the bank's new "address," which later turned out to be the address of Wolfram's Las Vegas condominium. The letters sent to box 24F were delivered to apartment 24F at the address. In the telegrammed reply, supposedly from the bank, all the bonds were accounted for, and the telegram ended with a message telling Bell & Beckwith to mail future confirmation letters to the new address. The clerk at the time did what seemed reasonable, not even suspecting that Wolfram himself had sent the telegram.

Wolfram had a close brush with the regulatory agencies in 1976, when the auditors at the time, Arthur Young & Co., issued a "material weakness" report that had to be relayed to the SEC. The report noted that Bell & Beckwith had too many incorrect customer statements and incomplete securities-verification counts. Arthur Young also said in its management letter to the Bell & Beckwith partners that year that Bell & Beckwith's volume was growing too fast for its antiquated posting system, and it recommended automation. And although Arthur Young didn't find the irregularities in Wolfram's accounts, it did warn that the firm needed to strengthen its internal controls.

Wolfram was a hard worker and a creature of habit. He would arrive in the office usually a little before or after 8:00 in the morning and would leave shortly after the market closed. He was never idle. When he wasn't on the phone, he was meeting with someone or working out the details of a deal. For years, he had a male secretary who had little to do because Wolfram took charge of every project that landed on his desk.

Wolfram almost always left for lunch at 11:30 and usually dined with the same companions—Frank McManus, his lifelong friend, neighbor, and attorney (McManus and Wolfram were the best man at each other's wedding), Roscoe Betz, and John Ayling. Besides the fact that Betz had been a friend since high school, Wolfram liked Betz because of their mutual interest in sports gambling and raising racehorses. He liked Ayling for several reasons—Ayling had been a basketball star at DeVilbiss High School in Toledo and later at the University of Toledo, and he was a deal maker. Ayling, a salesman for Bell & Beckwith, had repeatedly been asked to join the firm as a partner and always refused. On occasion, Wolfram sent up a trial balloon, suggesting that Ayling might be his successor as managing partner.

And Ayling had performed a couple of market coups that endeared him to Wolfram. In one of those deals, Ayling and Wolfram in effect cornered the market on stock of Acceleration Corp. in Columbus, Ohio, by buying expiring warrants for a nickel apiece and then exercising them. The company's stock went from $2\frac{3}{4}$ to around 8 in a few months, and Ayling's and Wolfram's 220,000 shares nearly tripled in value.

The lunchtime coterie had regular rounds to make. Every Thursday they went to Packo's, the east-side hot-dog place made famous by Jamie Farr (Corporal Klinger on TV's "M*A*S*H"); on Friday it was usually Arnie's, a saloon owned partly by Ayling, or the Golden Lily, a Chinese restaurant in downtown Toledo. Once in a while, they ventured out to Bud and Luke's, a working man's restaurant in the near downtown, or farther out to some of the popular business dining establishments like Mancy's and the Wooden Indian in Perrysburg.

At lunch the conversation almost always centered on sports and sports gambling, with a little business mixed in. Wolfram had a standing bet with Phil Roth, a Toledo furrier, for $200 a week—with each bettor alternating the game and the spread—but at times Wolfram bet as much as $10,000 on football or basketball games with professional bookies. Some of the bookies were bold enough to come into Bell & Beckwith's staid offices. The employees and partners were well aware of the sports gambling that went on, not only by Wolfram but also by several others in the firm. It was just another aspect of a busy day.

Wolfram would have legitimately made well over $100,000 and as much as $140,000 in a good year as a partner in the firm, and as managing partner, he drew an additional $25,000 a year. His adjusted gross incomes reported to the IRS for 1975 through 1980 were $164,000, a loss of $31,700, $62,000, a loss of $391,000, a loss of $93,000, and $170,000. (Those figures were warped by his illegal activities, however, and he had not filed final tax forms for 1981.)

The other seven general partners withdrew an average of $146,000 from their drawing accounts in Bell & Beckwith's final year of business. The withdrawals ranged from a low of $54,000 for Coon to a high of $272,000 for Betz and $220,000 for Jesionowski. In the final years of Bell & Beckwith, cracks had begun to show in the firm's foundation. Several partners left, partly because of their dislike of Wolfram's style. Among them were James Secor, grandson of one of the firm's founders (it was established as Secor & Bell in 1898 by Jay K. Secor and James B. Bell), and Louis Haubner, Jr., who managed the firm's branch office in Lima, Ohio.

Oddly, even with the incredible escalation of values and the increased chance of detection, Wolfram told investigators after he was caught that he had to spend only an average of 20 minutes a day on his paperwork manipulations. However, he said on the witness stand that his after-work hours were another thing.

During the sentencing hearing after Bell & Beckwith's collapse, Wolfram admitted that he had been a tormented man for months. "It is never a quiet moment

4

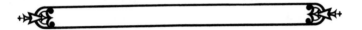

The Dragnet
Closes In

By Wednesday, February 2, nine days after he had begun his examination of Bell & Beckwith, Ralph Buie suspected that he might have happened onto a major fraud, but he needed final proof. By that time, too, Ted Wolfram was almost certain that he and the firm were in serious trouble. This examination wasn't going the way previous ones had. Buie, although a quiet, mild-mannered man, wasn't cowed by Wolfram's personality, nor was he overly impressed by Bell & Beckwith's prestige and reputation.

Buie was zeroing in on the damaging evidence, records that Wolfram had glibly explained away in many an audit and examination. The pressure was beginning to show on Wolfram's nerves. Uncharacteristically, Wolfram stayed late into the evening several times that week. By Thursday, Buie was almost certain that most, perhaps all, of the $383 million in collateral that backed Bell & Beckwith's margin accounts was nonexistent. Any one of the discrepancies could have been written off as simple human error, but there were too many discrepancies—and they all pointed to the same thing.

First there was a telegram with an incomplete sender's address. Then there was a verification letter (accounting for $105 million in bonds in a Nevada bank) without a bank stamp on it. A letter was dated with the wrong year in the heading. A check of transfer agents failed to turn up any of the bonds—at least under the names Wolfram had given Buie. And Wolfram couldn't locate a statement from Drexel Burnham Lambert that would account for the remaining collateral—Japanese stocks carried on the books at $278 million. When he finally produced the statement, it was a photocopy, and the figures didn't add correctly.

While Buie and the SEC were going through the necessary motions of subpoenaing the Las Vegas bank to get a physical count of the securities, and while they were obtaining an original statement from Drexel Burnham in New York, Wolfram was busy trying to buy time. He called some of the firm's best sales reps at home at night and told them that because of a temporary cash bind, he needed to raise additional deposits and would pay an extra 1 percent or 2 percent interest to attract the new money. He assured them that the firm was financially sound. He told one of the brokers that the cash bind had resulted from pledging a $10 million Treasury security to help save a New York bank—an investment he said would pay handsome dividends in the future.

Friday morning—on what was to be Bell & Beckwith's last day in business—events were hurrying by on several levels. Early that morning, Wolfram checked with several of the sales reps to see if any significant new cash deposits had come in. There were few. Wolfram knew then that he had only one chance to save the firm.

He realized that sooner or later the SEC would discover either that the $105 million in bonds didn't exist or that the $278 million in Japanese stock was grossly overstated. So he needed millions, perhaps $25 million, in new collateral to cover some of the larger margin accounts that had been used to finance such Wolfram enterprises as the Landmark Hotel, Country Boy Estates, and Arrowhead Exploration.

Wolfram decided to go to an old friend and business partner, Charles McKenny, for help. McKenny and his wife, Mary, had made millions on the sale of oil and gas properties, and the McKenny family had a total of more than $8 million invested in Bell & Beckwith alone. McKenny, a partner in the Toledo law firm of McKenny & Ernsberger, was also in partnership with Wolfram in several businesses—TZ Land & Cattle, Inc., Arrowhead Exploration Co., and the Arkansas farms.

Sometime on Friday, Wolfram and McKenny went to the main office of Toledo Trust Co. to meet with a senior vice-president. McKenny was well known around the bank, and he had no difficulty getting to a senior officer quickly.

Wolfram, on the other hand, had kept such a low profile in the Toledo business community that he was hardly known at all, even though Bell & Beckwith at one time had done some financing through Toledo Trust. Wolfram began the conversation by saying that he and the bank's president, George Haigh, were old friends. There was an element of truth in the remark: Haigh was a year behind Wolfram at Maumee High School, and they had known each other then. Wolfram told the banker that examiners were discounting some of his wife's holdings, and their recalcitrance had caused a temporary shortfall of more than $20 million in Bell & Beckwith's margin accounts.

McKenny said he was prepared to pledge $12 million to $13 million in securities if the bank would put up another $10 million to be backed by a second mortgage on the Landmark Hotel and Casino and the land on which it sat. That would make the total loan $22 million to $23 million.

Wolfram said he needed the money that day, or the next Monday at the latest, to solve the regulatory problem. But Wolfram did not have a financial statement with him (McKenny was so well known, he probably wouldn't have needed one), and the banker told him to bring a financial statement back on Monday morning. Actually, the banker had no intention of lending $10 million on the hotel without a thorough appraisal, but he didn't want to insult McKenny.

For Wolfram, Monday never came. Events on another level were already bringing Bell & Beckwith to the point of collapse.

The SEC subpoena presented to First Interstate Bank in Las Vegas that Friday morning yielded no bonds at all. And the photocopy of the Drexel Burnham statement of the Japanese stock had proved to be a forgery. So the SEC began hectic preparations for putting Bell & Beckwith out of business. Without telling Wolfram it was all over, Buie left the brokerage to get a plane back to Chicago, and he began drafting an affidavit to persuade a federal judge to issue a temporary restraining order to shut the firm down.

At Bell & Beckwith, it was business as usual, for everyone except Wolfram. One of the partners, Roscoe Betz, had lunch in Maumee with a young woman who wanted to join the firm as a broker. Robert Fox, a former partner who had left the firm and returned as a salesman, had a good day, making 40 trades worth at least $3,000 in commissions, and he knew he would have to come back Saturday to get caught up on paperwork.

Most of the staff were making weekend plans. Some were off to Michigan's ski resorts, just a few hours' drive from Toledo. For basketball fans, it promised to be an outstanding weekend: Televised games included some big college showdowns like Alabama at Kentucky, Iowa at Purdue, South Carolina at Notre Dame, and Michigan at Michigan State. Part 5 of the much-touted "Shogun" series was on television, competing with "The Dukes of Hazzard" for prime-time attention.

At the end of the day, around 5:00 or 5:30, John Ayling, one of the sales reps, decided to leave for the weekend. Although Ted Wolfram usually was gone by 4:00, he was still at his desk. As Ayling walked out, Wolfram said, "See you Monday." Ayling left with about $80 in his pocket. Roscoe Betz walked out with a Bell & Beckwith check for $125; it was the last money he would see from the firm, and just over a year later, he was to declare Chapter 11 bankruptcy. At the end of its last day in business, Bell & Beckwith's cash drawer had $52.17 in it.

Late that afternoon in Las Vegas, the performers for Zula Productions, Zula Wolfram's show-production company at the Landmark Hotel and Casino, were preparing for their busiest time of the week, the weekend performances of "Spellcaster" in the Empire Room and a separate musical show in the Galaxy Lounge.

Theodore Focht, general counsel (and now president) of the Securities Investor Protection Corp., left his Washington, D.C., office a little after 5:00 and headed for his suburban Virginia home. He had known for several days that there was some sort of problem with Bell & Beckwith, and he knew that an SEC team had flown to Las Vegas to look into some bonds. But he had assumed the examination was nothing out of the ordinary until that Friday, when the SEC told him a subpoena was being served on a Las Vegas bank that supposedly held the bonds for Bell & Beckwith.

Focht had just sat down to supper when the phone

rang. "My God, Ted, would you believe the bank did give us information and the information is they had no account like that?" the man from the SEC told Focht.

By then, the SEC regarded the Bell & Beckwith situation as an emergency requiring fast court action to preserve the assets that were left. Focht was asked if he could fly to Toledo by Saturday morning. He couldn't get out of Washington that quickly, but he called in a couple of secretaries to begin typing adjudication documents and authorizations for SIPC's board of directors, and he set about tracking down at least four of the seven directors needed for the authorization to proceed on a case.

Late that evening in Toledo, U.S. District Court Judge Nicholas Walinski went to bed knowing that he might have a shocker of a case on his hands. Walinski, a longtime political figure around the Lucas County courthouse, had gotten his federal judgeship as a Nixon appointee 13 years before the Bell & Beckwith affair and had handled no nationally prominent cases. But this one had to be a big case—Walinski had already been told that the losses could exceed $20 million or even $30 million (both estimates were low, because in the scramble to get the case filed quickly, the SEC examiner had not yet discovered a $15 million margin account that escalated the loss figure).

Early on the morning of Saturday, February 5, Wolfram called his family together and reached his parents by telephone in Las Vegas, where they were vacationing. He told them he had taken money from Bell & Beckwith and that he would have to take the consequences. Then he and his wife left for the ten-minute drive to Toledo Express Airport for the hearing.

It was one of the strangest hearings in Judge Walinski's 25 years on the bench. Because the federal courthouse was closed on Saturday and Walinski couldn't open it on such short notice, he arranged the hearing at the airport for the convenience of the SEC contingent flying in from Chicago that morning. One of the SEC lawyers found a vacant conference room at the Airport Motel, across the parking lot from the main terminal.

During the long hearing, lawyers from the SEC and lawyers representing Bell & Beckwith frequently asked for private conferences, and Walinski would leave the room to have a cup of coffee while the attorneys argued. Ralph Buie, the examiner who started the chain of events that led to the hearing, had worked into the night on his affidavit, and several times he answered Walinski's questions. It was a busy Saturday—Buie's four-page affidavit was followed by a ten-page motion and complaint from the SEC and a five-page memorandum. And by shortly after 4:00 that afternoon, Judge Walinski responded with a five-page temporary restraining order.

Even before the hearing started, Judge Walinski was so sure of Bell & Beckwith's insolvency (on the basis of the preliminary report from the SEC) that he called Joseph Shibley—a Toledo attorney who had worked as a court receiver on a number of occasions—and asked him to go to the airport and stand by. Long before the actual order was filed, at 4:19, Shibley was working on the security of Bell & Beckwith's main office downtown.

About 12:30 that Saturday, Bob Fox stopped off at Bell & Beckwith to finish his paperwork. He noticed Donald Henninger, the firm's controller, talking to two or three dark-suited men in the back, apparently working on the computer system. After 20 minutes, Fox walked toward the back of the brokerage and made a flip remark to Henninger about the extra help, but Henninger didn't laugh.

Fox went back to his desk, and after another 10 or 15 minutes, he heard a tap at the front door, and three more people came in—two men in suits and a woman, all with briefcases. The three immediately went upstairs to the boardroom. Within a few minutes, three more men joined them.

By this time, Fox knew something was drastically wrong. He asked one of the strangers what was going on, and the answer was that he'd know in due time. Another of the men remarked, matter of factly, that Bell & Beckwith was finished. Fox was almost in a state of shock. After a few minutes, he called his wife and told her to tell their friends—with whom they had a dinner date—that he was ill.

Henninger, pale and shaken, came up to Fox's desk and sat across from him. Henninger told Fox that Judge Walinski had convened a special court hearing at the airport—a hearing involving the SEC, the NYSE, federal marshals, and lots of other people.

A short while later, Shibley, the newly appointed temporary trustee, walked into the brokerage and told the employees—Fox, Henninger, and one or two others—that he had been named to take possession of Bell & Beckwith's property. About half an hour later, a guard appeared, and a locksmith began changing the locks on the doors. Fox got up to leave, and the guard and Shibley told him to empty his pockets.

Later that evening, after locking up the Defiance office, Barry Sucher prepared to go out for the evening. He was planning to drive to Toledo to a fancy riverfront restaurant named Ricardo's, the payoff for a football bet. He was still drying off from his shower when the phone rang. The call was from a friend in another Toledo brokerage who said he had heard from an attorney that Bell & Beckwith was in trouble and was being shut down by federal marshals.

Sucher couldn't believe what he had heard. He called Bell & Beckwith's Toledo office and asked for Bob

Fox, knowing that Fox often stopped in the office on Saturdays. "I'm sorry, he can't come to the phone," Sucher was told. "Who can't come to the phone?" Sucher asked. And the reply was: "No one can come to the phone." Sucher, too sick at that point to care about eating, dressed, got in his Mercedes, and drove to Toledo for his dinner date anyway.

He was among the first to know of the Bell & Beckwith disaster, but before the end of the weekend, many others would find out.

5

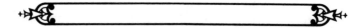

The Bomb Drops
on Toledo

The rumors of a disaster at Bell & Beckwith mounted over the weekend, so that by Monday morning, February 7, it was clear something was wrong.

An executive of the *Blade* had talked to a friend at Drexel Burnham Lambert in New York and knew about the SEC's inquiry into the phony Toto statement. The executive relayed the information to the *Blade*'s city desk, and on Sunday night several reporters tried unsuccessfully to get comments from some of the Bell & Beckwith partners. But just the fact that no one was willing to talk caused suspicion to deepen.

Early on Monday morning, a team of *Blade* reporters went to work on the problem again. One reporter began assembling a history of Bell & Beckwith, working with clippings that were so ancient they literally fell apart as they were being read. Another began calling the SEC and the New York Stock Exchange. Still another reporter took the four-block walk to Bell & Beckwith's building in the bitter February cold, making his way through the three inches of snow that had fallen on the city overnight to see firsthand whether the firm would open for business that morning.

At first, SEC and NYSE officials wouldn't comment, other than to say an announcement was pending. Then, with the presses already rolling for the newspaper's first edition, the story that would shock Toledo began to fall into place. Shortly before 9:00 A.M. the New York Stock Exchange issued a terse press release: "The New York Stock Exchange said that Bell & Beckwith of Toledo, Ohio, has been summarily suspended as a member organization effective prior to the opening of business today. The exchange has found the organization to be in such financial difficulty that it cannot be permitted to do business as a member organization."

The reporter who went to the Bell & Beckwith building on Erie Street met the same response, as did dozens of Bell & Beckwith customers—the plate-glass doors were locked, and a guard occasionally opened them slightly to tell customers that the building was closed. Telephone callers found either no answer or a busy signal; and the busy signals came so frequently that Ohio Bell Telephone Co. sent technicians to investigate the problem. One young couple turned away at the door said their savings to buy a house were in a cash account at Bell & Beckwith, and another customer said he had driven downtown to make a withdrawal to pay off a large loan. Many other customers complained to the guard, to reporters, to anyone who would listen, that their life savings were tied up in the firm, that they had already written checks that might bounce, or that they had options that would soon expire.

By midmorning, the *Blade* had replated its front page to add a boldface headline in the upper right corner of page 1:

NYSE Suspends Bell & Beckwith; Firm Is Closed

Brokerage's Financial Ills Cited

The front-page story gave the details of the suspension by the New York Stock Exchange, sketchy reports on events of the preceding weekend (the temporary restraining order issued by Judge Nicholas Walinski and the appointment of a temporary receiver), and the announcement that the Securities Investor Protection Corp. had requested a hearing to consider the appointment of a permanent trustee.

The second edition of the *Blade* went to press around 10:30, and by noon copies of the paper were being circulated in the popular gathering places of Toledo's business elite—the Toledo Club, Toledo Country Club, Belmont Country Club, Sylvania Country Club, Inverness Club, and such restaurants as Dyer's Chop House downtown.

By noon the story had broken on every radio and television station in town, too, and it was the topic of conversation everywhere. Some people had reason to be more interested than others. Word had already started to spread that Bell & Beckwith's cash accounts could be in a "special" category and therefore might not be fully insured.

Even before the media got the full story to the general public, behind-the-scenes events were occurring that led to stories that would shock newspaper readers and television viewers even more in the next several days.

At 9:00 that Monday morning, the sales reps for Bell & Beckwith, by then totally confused, gathered for coffee and rolls at the Sheraton Westgate Inn to explore a problem they didn't understand and to try to answer questions they couldn't even formulate at the time. Unbeknownst to them, at that precise moment, in the federal courtroom chambers halfway across town, Judge Walinski was meeting with a small group of lawyers representing the brokerage and with Theodore Focht, general counsel for the Securities Investor Protection Corp. The judge's meeting was fairly brief, because by that time he was convinced there was clear evidence of Ted Wolfram's theft, and he knew there was little chance of saving the firm.

Patrick A. McGraw, an attorney with Fuller & Henry who was to play a very important role in the case in the ensuing months, came to work that morning under the impression that it was a normal day. McGraw, a Phi Beta Kappa Democrat—with an honors degree in political science from Kenyon College and a Harvard law degree—was, at 40, a few years older than most of his fellow lawyers. The firm he worked in had an undeserved reputation for stodginess, a reputation derived largely from the clients it represented (Owens-Illinois, Inc. and Toledo Edison Co., among others). McGraw had had considerable experience working on stock and bond offerings for Owens-Illinois, a big glass and packaging company, and for the utility.

At midmorning John McHugh III, a trial lawyer with Fuller & Henry, came into McGraw's office and said, "It's all over the street. The SEC has shut down Bell & Beckwith." Shortly after McHugh left McGraw's office,

Randolph Light rushed in. Light, managing partner of Fuller & Henry at the time, had just been contacted by SIPC's Ted Focht. "I just got off the phone with a guy named Focht from SIPC. Do you know what SIPC is?" he asked McGraw excitedly. McGraw recalled that SIPC was somewhat similar to the FDIC (which insures banks) but that was all he knew about it.

Within a few minutes, a meeting was called with Focht, McGraw, Light, and Thomas Dalrymple, another attorney with Fuller & Henry. Focht made it clear that Fuller & Henry was not the only firm under consideration for the assignment, an assignment that would eventually be one of the most lucrative in Toledo's legal history.

Focht had spent the weekend studying up on Ohio's law firms. He had done business previously with a large Cleveland firm, and he knew that if he couldn't find a Toledo firm capable of handling the big case, he could go to Cleveland for help. But he preferred to deal with one more intimately familiar with Toledo politics. The firm he would choose had to be large enough to handle the burden of litigating a case insolving $20 million, $30 million, or even $40 million in losses. All these considerations narrowed the choice to perhaps four or five in Toledo, and one of those—Shumaker, Loop & Kendrick—was out of contention because of a conflict of interest, in that it represented Bell & Beckwith.

While Focht was wrestling with the problem of who SIPC would choose to take charge of what would surely be a long legal battle, other events were making the case even more important.

Ralph Buie, the SEC examiner who had uncovered the fraud, went back into the Bell & Beckwith building to continue his examination and discovered a computer printout of a $15 million margin account that hadn't shown up the previous week. That account took the amount of the insolvency from the $21 million range up to $36 million—and increased the amount of the fraud from $32 million to $47 million (the actual shortage was $51 million before assets were taken into consideration).

Late on Monday afternoon, Focht invited some reporters from the *Blade* to his room at the Holiday Inn Riverview downtown to offer assurances that most investors could expect to get their money back. He said the process could take as little as a month or as long as several months. Focht did not know at the time but soon became aware that the Bell & Beckwith case was different from prior brokerage failures in that many of the 7,000 accounts involved cash deposits that couldn't automatically be regarded as being held for trading purposes. SIPC, a quasi-governmental agency created by Congress in 1970, insures brokerage customers up to a total of $500,000 each, including a maximum of $100,000 cash. But SIPC guarantees cash deposits only if the cash is "for the purpose of purchasing securities." And its rules specifically say that "cash balances maintained solely for the purpose of earning interest are not protected." (See the Appendix for more detailed information on SIPC's rules.)

The big problem in the Bell & Beckwith case was determining how many of the cash accounts were truly for the purpose of securities trading. Many of the investors were lured by the fact that Bell & Beckwith was offering substantially higher interest rates than most other brokerages, and many of the customers had not made a single stock trade months after placing their deposits. A harsh interpretation of the situation could have labeled those accounts as "subordinated" deposits, and therefore not covered by SIPC's insurance.

Depending on how the decision went, hundreds of Bell & Beckwith customers could have lost millions of dollars. But perhaps because Bell & Beckwith was one of the first brokerage firms to fail in the money-market era of the 1980s, the rules were liberally interpreted. In fact, because of a partial distribution of liquidated assets in 1984, some account holders with $400,000 or more in cash received all but a fraction—say, $50,000—of their cash back.

SIPC's rules themselves, written before interest rates spiraled in the late 1970s and early 1980s and before the money market became more attractive than the stock market, left a way out: "SIPC presumes that cash balances are left in securities accounts for the purpose of purchasing securities. It would require substantial evidence to the contrary to overcome this presumption. Standing alone, the fact that a cash balance was earning interest and was not used to purchase securities for a considerable period of time—say, four or five months—would not be sufficient to overcome the presumption."

On Tuesday, Shumaker, Loop & Kendrick, attorneys for Bell & Beckwith, filed a statement at the Lucas County courthouse—signed by Ted and Zula Wolfram— that assigned the Wolframs' property to Bell & Beckwith. It covered "all accounts . . . all partnership interests and other rights to payment of any kind; all notes, instruments and documents of title; all consumer goods; all inventory; all equipment; all general intangibles; and all horses, and all interests in all horses and syndications of horses . . . [including] interests in Country Boy Estates, 1360 135th Street, Ocala, Florida."

After the document was filed, an attorney with Shumaker, Loop told a *Blade* reporter that Wolfram also had resigned as managing partner. That piece of information, reported in the newspaper, caused Judge Walinski to impose a rare gag order barring lawyers from issuing any statements about the case other than those made in court. Walinski's reasoning was that statements outside the court might jeopardize the value of the property and force a "distress-sale" liquidation. By Wednesday, Focht had made his decision. Pat McGraw would be the liquidation trustee, but he decided not to make it official until the next day.

But by Thursday morning, February 10, McGraw was sufficiently confident of becoming trustee that he began interviewing officers of some of the city's big accounting firms. Toledo, which is home to six *Fortune* 500 companies (Dana Corp., Champion Spark Plug Co., Sheller-Globe Corp., and three big glass companies: Libbey-Owens-Ford Co., Owens-Corning Fiberglas Corp., and Owens-Illinois), also is represented by most of the Big Eight accounting firms.

McGraw spent most of Thursday interviewing the accountants, and by the end of the day Judge Walinski had signed the consent order naming McGraw the trustee. Walinski had originally set a hearing date for Friday, so it was unnecessary to sign the order that quickly. But he felt there was no point in delaying it. He also decided that, having announced the Friday hearing, he would proceed as scheduled but would turn the hearing into an information meeting for the investors and for the press. He sensed that the community was in a state of shock over the Bell & Beckwith disaster, and he wanted to release as much information as possible to allay any fears.

And there were some real fears. The newspapers and radio and TV stations had speculated that some of the Bell & Beckwith accounts might be in danger of being considered subordinated loans and therefore not subject to reimbursement. But along with a great deal of confusion over the whole business, there were some notes of optimism. Several large brokerages announced that they were going to bid for Bell & Beckwith's accounts, which, after all, represented a sizable chunk of the city's well-heeled

59

investors. And the Bell & Beckwith partners were still bravely trying to find a buyer for the entire business (at that point they didn't know that Wolfram's property, including the hotel and the horse farm, wouldn't come close to satisfying the deficit). Even SIPC, which at least knew the amount of the shortage, was still officially saying that liquidation was not certain—the agency, publicly anyway, was holding out hope for a last-minute miracle to save the firm.

Readers of the *Blade* that Thursday evening got a preview of what was to come in Friday's court session. An editorial titled "Breaking a Brokerage" presaged the bankruptcy:

> The sudden collapse of Bell & Beckwith, Toledo's oldest brokerage firm, has sent shock waves through the community that will ripple on for months.
>
> The full story of what went on at this venerable stock house has not yet emerged. But what little is known thus far indicates that this is a financial scandal of the first order, involving some $36 million in alleged shortages, missing and intentionally overvalued securities, and myriad practices in violation of rules and regulations of the security industry.
>
> It is particularly sad to countless Toledoans of an earlier generation that the doors at Bell & Beckwith had to be closed in this fashion. Many had become staunch and devoted customers of the firm, which they held in high regard. The brokerage was respected, both for its professionalism and for the personal touch its personnel brought to the impersonal business of buying and selling securities.
>
> Many a customer—large and small—recalls the universally warm welcome with which the firm's representatives greeted all comers. Female customers in particular were courted at a time when brokerage houses were mainly male bastions. There would be occasional corsages for the ladies, doughnuts and cider in season, bags of peanuts for one and all, and more. The aim was to make one feel wanted and at home even as the mundane subject of investments was being dusted off.

And in that editorial, the *Blade* raised a question that may be the most lingering issue in the Bell & Beckwith case—an issue that, in some ways, could rewrite investigatory and enforcement procedures:

> That a financial collapse of this scope can happen underscores the need for constant scrutiny of the operations of companies dealing in billions of dollars of other people's money. The Securities and Exchange Commission did move swiftly to clamp a lock on Bell & Beckwith the moment serious shortages became evident. The question always will be why earlier audits did not show that something was amiss.
>
> What this boils down to is that an established, respected brokerage house was brought down by the human frailties and avarice of one or more individuals. And when one partner can so dominate a company as to have almost a free rein, it reflects sadly on the management acumen of the others.
>
> This failure is an isolated aberration, confined to a single . firm. It should not be used for a minute to tarnish or diminish the honesty and integrity of the securities industry as a whole or of other firms doing business in this city. This is a woeful day in Toledo's financial history; brighter days, we trust, are ahead.

About 8:00 that Thursday—the evening before the first public hearing—Pat McGraw came to the conclusion that on the basis of its ability to do the enormous task, its ability to gear up for the undertaking quickly, and the fee required, the firm of Ernst & Whinney would get the accounting assignment.

And it did. By the morning of Friday, February 11, Ernst & Whinney had 20 employees on the scene at Bell & Beckwith to begin the laborious task of sorting through the records of the 7,000 account holders. Many of the 20 professionals were imported overnight from assignments in other cities. One of the primary reasons McGraw chose Ernst & Whinney was the firm's expertise with electronics. McGraw had the feeling that it would be necessary to "break the code" to extract meaningful data from Bell & Beckwith's computer system.

When the hearing convened on Friday, about 120 people, many of whom didn't know that Bell & Beckwith was totally bankrupt, crowded into the federal courtroom—occupying all the available seats, standing in the aisles, and sitting in the jury box. There had been much talk in the community of somehow saving the firm or reopening it under new management with new financing. But Walinski quickly dispelled any such notions.

As far as the general public was concerned, the Bell & Beckwith case was only four days old, but it was all over in a few minutes that Friday. Judge Walinski confirmed the worst fear—that the firm was insolvent, that liquidation was the only possibility. Walinski told the courtroom that in 25 years on the bench he had never seen a case move so swiftly, and he said that the speed of the proceedings might have averted a financial disaster for the community. Judge Walinski said that he was moving the case to bankruptcy court and that a trustee had been appointed. Then, in a rare move, he opened the courtroom to questions from the audience.

Several investors took advantage of the offer. One man told the crowded courtroom that he felt as though he had been robbed with a paper pistol. The judge assured him that the FBI and the district attorney's office were investigating possible criminal action. Another investor asked who was going to pay the legal fees in the case. The answer: ultimately, the assets of the firm, not the taxpayers.

Judge Walinski assured the audience that "not many people are going to be hurt, except possibly the partners." (In Ohio, each general partner is liable for the entire loss in case of a business failure.) The judge went on to say that he expected only minor losses among the public. "I don't think anyone will be wiped out," he declared. Later, however, it became clear that some investors would suffer major losses. One family, for instance, had a grand total of $8 million in various Bell & Beckwith accounts, far in excess of SIPC limits.

The judge introduced the newly named trustee, Pat McGraw, and the man from SIPC, Ted Focht, and he assigned the bankruptcy case to Judge Walter Krasniewski (who later withdrew because a relative had an account at the firm). Both Focht and McGraw made short speeches—McGraw vowing that he would begin a diligent search for the firm's assets and Focht explaining in brief the complicated SIPC asset-distribution formula that would cost many Toledoans hours of reading time in the coming months.

Essentially, Focht told the audience that customers with securities in their own names would get back all their stocks as soon as possible; that those with "street-name" securities at the brokerage would receive a pro rata share of the assets (after the assets were combined into a fund of customer property), and that all other assets of the firm would go toward payment of the noncustomer creditors.

It was over almost as quickly as it had begun. With the bankruptcy a fact, the proud old firm was wiped out. And trustee McGraw was about to start on a search for assets that would take him and his crew literally to the far reaches of the continent.

Just as the newspaper predicted, shock waves did indeed ripple through the community. The paranoia in the city is illustrated by what happened to Sylvania Savings Bank, a small institution based in the Toledo suburb of Sylvania. Two weeks after the collapse of Bell & Beckwith, the bank was jeopardized by a run after rumors began circulating that it had made a sizable bad loan to the brokerage. Sylvania Savings was faced with long lines of depositors wanting to withdraw their money. It took four days for the bank to get back to normal business.

6

Picking Up the Pieces

Even before Bell & Beckwith was officially placed in bankruptcy, trustee Patrick McGraw was working nearly round the clock to secure the various Bell & Beckwith properties, and he had already embarked on a trail of assets unlike those encountered in a "normal" brokerage failure.

In addition to the usual rich man's baubles, the trustee had found such Wolfram assets as a Las Vegas hotel-casino, a horse farm in Florida, oil and gas properties, cattle ranches, a high-rise condominium in Las Vegas, a $2 million jet, and a stableful of cars that would have made a sheikh envious.

In addition, McGraw and as many as 20 accountants and specialists from Ernst & Whinney, the accounting firm chosen to assist in the liquidation, faced the formidable task of sorting through the seemingly hopeless tangle of records for the 7,000 investors. On paper, the firm and its customers had assets of nearly $110 million, but it was obvious that its actual assets were worth many millions—up to $40 million—less than that.

It will take years to resolve the case, and lawsuits totaling hundreds of millions of dollars have already been filed, long before the conclusion of the case. An indication of the complexity of the Bell & Beckwith bankruptcy came 21 months after the scandal broke, when the trustee filed a 1,045-page report detailing the assets known at that point. In addition to listing the holdings of each customer, the report included some Bell & Beckwith trivia—for example, that there were 189 slot machines in the Landmark Hotel and Casino when the brokerage collapsed.

McGraw, a quiet, personable man, eventually would make enemies because of his deliberately slow, by-the-numbers disposition of some assets and his haste in getting rid of others—and because of decisions that necessarily favored some categories of creditors over others and, in effect, pitted partner against partner. (Sometimes McGraw was criticized for the wrong reasons. He sold one of Wolfram's horses for $50,000, for example, and soon afterward the horse—which had been ailing—made a rapid recovery and won a $200,000 race. McGraw was assailed by an attorney in court but was defended by the bankruptcy judge, who said that "the trustee in a bankruptcy is not in a position to be speculative.")

Even before the news of the collapse had fully set in, Bell & Beckwith's employees and partners were trying to refashion their lives.

Edward Esgain, a former general partner who had been retired for 11 years but who was still a limited partner with about $30,000 at risk in Bell & Beckwith, was enjoying a vacation at a hotel in Florida the day the story of the firm's collapse hit *The Wall Street Journal*. Esgain's son-in-law in Cleveland called him excitedly to relate the news. Esgain immediately settled his hotel bill, packed, and left for Toledo, fearing the worst for his limited-partnership share. Esgain, who had worked his way up from cashier to become a general partner, was in such a hurry to get back to Toledo that he damaged the transmission of his car and had to pay nearly $900 to get it repaired en route.

Barry Sucher, manager of Bell & Beckwith's branch office in Defiance, Ohio, was lucky enough to have duplicate copies, at home, of some of his customers' records. For weeks he did business—selling for a former competitor, Cleveland-based Prescott, Ball & Turben—from his home's sunporch.

The Monday that Bell & Beckwith failed to open, Robert Fox, a former partner of the firm who had left and rejoined as a salesman, took more than 100 calls at his home from customers who were confused and angered by the closing. Fox, luckier than many of the Bell & Beckwith employees, shortly made a deal with Cowen & Co. in New York to open a Toledo office, with Fox as manager—in the hope of salvaging much of Bell & Beckwith's customer list. Two weeks after the collapse of Bell & Beckwith, Fox and a dozen of the firm's former employees (including four general partners) were sitting in Fort Industry Square—in the same space that was to have been Bell & Beckwith's new offices—going page by page through the Toledo telephone book trying to reconstruct, from memory, the 7,000 names on the firm's customer list, by then locked securely in its defunct quarters on Erie Street, four blocks away.

At the same time, John Ayling, another salesman for Bell & Beckwith, was striking a deal with Chicago-based Oberweis Securities with the same idea in mind. He, too, had lined up several former partners and employees. And, simultaneously, Prescott, Ball & Turben, Paine Webber, and Kidder Peabody, among others, were trying to persuade the trustee to turn over the Bell & Beckwith accounts to them in bulk (they eventually went to Oberweis).

By the second week in March, more than a month after the collapse of Bell & Beckwith, there was still great uncertainty in Toledo about the "special" cash accounts and whether they would be covered by SIPC insurance.

The media were bombarded with questions and

comments on the case. Many investors wrote to the *Blade*, and by the hundreds they called the newspaper and the radio and TV stations. Trustee McGraw received thousands of letters, and his special telephone lines in Fuller & Henry's law offices sometimes required as many as five people to keep track of the calls. Many Toledoans obviously were angry, hurt, and disillusioned by the Bell & Beckwith collapse, and they wanted to tell about the hardships brought on their families because their accounts had already been tied up for more than a month. Some said their faith in the system had been shaken by the experience.

One woman who called the *Blade*, her voice shaking with anger, said: "We thought Bell & Beckwith was the safest place on earth, the Rock of Gibraltar. . . . We wanted it nice and safe for our retirement. . . . I really feel we were deceived. We're not starving or anything, but this has been a traumatic experience."

A man calling from his hospital bed after open-heart surgery asked: "What do we have to believe in? I don't know what to do anymore." The man said he and his four sons all had cash accounts at Bell & Beckwith. "I talked my sons into investing. It makes me sick."

Another man, the father of college-age children, bemoaned the fact that he had consolidated all his holdings in one Bell & Beckwith account just a couple of months before the collapse.

The stories coming into Pat McGraw's office in Edison Plaza were similar. From all the inquiries, he collected several dozen hardship cases for special attention. The other letters were read—some by several people—and all eventually were answered.

There were several patterns to the letters to McGraw—elderly people who were alone and living on very limited incomes; students and parents of students facing

tuition and dormitory bills; customers who had made purchases and who had counted on part of their Bell &
Beckwith holdings to make the payment or down payment;
and recently divorced women whose incomes were largely
dependent on their brokerage accounts.

McGraw told the press that his options were limited, and he was reluctant to talk about specific remedies
for the hardship cases. "For many persons, a kind of
healing is just talking about it," the *Blade* quoted him as
saying, "Just knowing someone cares."

In some cases, he reassured callers or letter writers
that their money was safe. For example, a church had
planned a large expansion project, costing about $500,000,
and its building fund had a substantial deposit at Bell &
Beckwith. The pastor wanted to present the plans to the
congregation, but he feared that the project was jeopardized by the brokerage failure. McGraw assured him the
account would probably be O.K., and the church went
ahead with its groundbreaking.

A widow with about $60,000 in a cash account wrote
to McGraw: "It's all the money I have—no other income at
all." A man wrote that he needed his money to help
support a brother who was mentally retarded and required
extraordinary attention.

An elderly Sylvania woman wrote: "The Bell &
Beckwith closing came to me as the most shocking news
ever. . . . I am disabled. . . . I'm very upset emotionally,
and, because of this, my physical condition is deteriorat-
ing."

A woman whose husband's only income was a mod-
est amount of strike pay told McGraw that she was due to
have a baby. "How do we pay bills and eat?" she asked.
"Now what do we do? How do we live?"

A man in his eighties, whose wife was also over 80,
wrote: "I believe it to be literally a matter of life and death.

Neither of us is able to sleep." McGraw talked to them and made some suggestions to put them at ease.

Many, even a majority, of the hardship cases were customers with relatively small amounts of money in Bell & Beckwith—which nonetheless were perhaps their life savings. To allay those fears, McGraw issued a press statement on March 9:

> Bell and Beckwith's cash accounts have been the subject of continuing study both here in Toledo and at the Securities Investor Protection Corp. I am pleased to say that I have been advised by SIPC that it will be providing coverage to virtually all eligible Bell & Beckwith cash accounts—subject to the statutory cash coverage limit of $100,000. While each individual claim must, of course, be handled on its own merits, the only cases where there might not be SIPC coverage would be those, if any, in which no evidence at all is available to show that the cash had been deposited for the purpose of purchasing securities. It appears quite likely that such evidence will be available to support SIPC coverage in most, if not all, cases. Where more than one account is held under closely related circumstances, such as two or more accounts in an individual family unit, it *may* be necessary to apply the $100,000 cash limit to the total amount in all closely related accounts. The trustee and SIPC will be continuing to analyze these kinds of cases, on an account-by-account basis, to determine how the $100,000 limit applies under each particular set of circumstances.

By March 16, nearly six weeks after Bell & Beckwith's demise, there were still enough questions about the handling of whole categories of claims that nearly 200 creditors, mostly investors, showed up at a hearing held for space reasons at a Masonic temple near downtown Toledo. It was a long meeting, lasting 4½ hours. At times during the creditors' meeting, dozens of hands were in the air as investors sought to be recognized. Eventually, the investors were limited to a single question apiece so that everyone could get the floor.

Trustee McGraw told the assemblage that Ernst & Whinney had been working overtime since the firm came on the case February 10. "We all began work immediately, and I do mean immediately, at nine o'clock at night," he said. ". . . Ernst & Whinney—and I'm not talking about one or two people; I'm talking about 12 or 15 people—are working on two 12-hour shifts on an around-the-clock basis."

McGraw went on to tell them that the transfer of Bell & Beckwith accounts, in bulk, to Oberweis was not going as smoothly as anticipated. "Some unexpected problems have been encountered in that process, and with the timing of that process," he said. He noted that a snag had developed in the entry of data in the computer of Swiss American Securities, Inc. (a securities firm that acted as a processor for Oberweis under contract).

A number of questions had to do with cash-account coverage, and at one point in the hearing, an investor threw a direct challenge at McGraw:

IRA KANNELL: My account—my wife['s] and my account is a cash account. I'm not going to try to kid anybody, and I won't lie on the claims forms and try to commit—or try to convince [people of] something that is not true. Now, as I understand it [for] a cash account under the folder that we were sent, there's no coverage. I'd like a clarification on that. You're saying it is covered; I'd like to know where it comes from.

McGRAW: Well, it depends on the facts, sir. Your folder—are you talking about the red SIPC folder?—doesn't say that cash isn't covered. It says that cash is covered under some circumstances.

KANNELL: The circumstances in this particular case, this is a cash account. It is not with—there was no intent on our part to buy securities.

McGRAW: The question is one of intent and how that can be shown, or of the origin of the money. If the money was money that resulted from the sale of securities, there may be coverage. But I don't know what more to tell you. I don't want to stand here and turn down your claim in a meeting. It doesn't make any sense for me to do that, sir.

(Kannell and his wife, Marilyn, got back their cash, nearly $35,000.)

Many of the questions went unanswered because of the ground rules—questions such as "How could $36 million be skimmed off?" "How could Bell & Beckwith get away with this for so long?" "Who blew the whistle?"

The trustee also drew pointed questions on the handling of options (under the rules, options were closed out as of the date of the firm's last day in business). One customer, Edith Kellner of Lima, Ohio, questioned Mc-Graw at length about the practice of closing out options. She wanted to know where the certificates were physically located. And she demanded to know "what right you have to close out an account which would not have been handled that way by me. What gives you a right to give me a loss?"

Stephen Harbeck, assistant general counsel of SIPC, answered, "Ma'am, options are a wasting asset."

"Not in my case it wasn't," Mrs. Kellner replied, and the audience laughed. Even though the meeting was long, the dialog was spirited at times, and the audience seemed to be caught up in it. "I've been in business 30 years, over 30 years, and I understand the procedure," Mrs. Kellner said.

Harbeck pointed out that everyone who deals in options receives a prospectus from the Options Clearing Corp. that points out that one of the risks of options is the possibility of losing control over assets in case of a failure.

Other creditors used the meeting to vent their

feelings about a variety of topics. One told of the hardships faced by some small-business owners who had been using Bell & Beckwith's cash accounts, with their attractive interest rates, for business deposits.

DAVID LAHEY: I'm paying $700 a month interest on money to operate [to replace money] that's laid down in Bell & Beckwith. Can I file a claim for that $700 a month interest?

McGRAW: This is interest, what, that accrued on your account before the firm closed?

LAHEY: I'm borrowing money to operate on unsecured loans.

McGRAW: This is money you're going to pay to a bank on money to be borrowed to operate your business?

LAHEY: Right.

McGRAW: I wish we had some way of compensating you for that, but we don't. The law doesn't allow it.

Some of the customers had even larger concerns, since their accounts were well over the SIPC limits. One man, in particular, occupied the floor on several occasions, for perhaps a total of half an hour, with his complicated problem. A portion of the exchange—at times sounding like doublespeak or some sort of convoluted foreign language—went as follows:

THOMAS DURNELL: My account would run pretty close to a million dollars. Now, I had a debit balance of $400,000, approximate figures. . . . Now I said to you, well, what about my security position, what about my income tax, which would be tremendous with a very low cost on my shares, since I had a very large position in one stock? . . . I'm told that I need an attorney when I don't see what's complicated about this thing. . . . Why would there be any reason why the debit balance would not move along with the $500,000 from SIPC?

Toward the end of the drawn-out creditors' meeting, one customer, Helen Abraham, summed up the feeling of many in the audience: ". . . How can people know what to do, whether to move from where they're living because they can't afford it if they don't get their money back? Nothing that you're telling me today reassures me of anything. I won't believe it till I see it right in my hand."

All the endless legal, financial, and criminal work involved with the Bell & Beckwith fraud—the depositions, the investors' hearings, the meetings with accountants, and the long preparation needed to bring the case to court— immediately affected Pat McGraw. For two or three weeks after McGraw was appointed trustee to liquidate Bell & Beckwith, he got by on three to four hours of sleep a night and kept close to 40 people working on the case, about half of them from Fuller & Henry and the other half accountants and computer and security specialists.

McGraw got so wrapped up in the case that he had to be reminded to eat, and several nights he didn't go home at all. On the nights when he did go home, he arrived after his wife, son, and daughter were already asleep and left before they got up. At one point, early in the case, he called the police chief in the bedroom community of Ottawa Hills and asked that the police department keep an eye on his children on their way to and from school.

Securing the physical property at the four Bell & Beckwith locations was one of the first tasks, begun at the downtown Toledo brokerage house minutes after Judge Walinski signed the order to enjoin Bell & Beckwith from doing business. But it was nearly a week later before locks were changed at all the locations.

Fuller & Henry had several attorneys working on

the security problem as soon as McGraw was officially appointed as trustee. On February 11 Fuller & Henry sent a representative to the Findlay office and the Defiance office, each about 45 miles outside of Toledo, and the next day a representative was sent to the Lima office, about 90 miles away.

Each encountered a different set of problems. In Defiance, for example, Bell & Beckwith's building was half-owned by Barry Sucher, the broker in charge. Sucher, claiming that Bell & Beckwith had defaulted on the partnership agreement, wanted to reopen as a broker for another firm. (He eventually did, but not until the building went through the same security precautions as the other locations.)

Glenn Rambo filed this report on his visit to the Findlay office:

> On Feb. 11, 1983, at approximately 11:00 A.M., I met Bill Phillips of Bill's Lock Service at the office of Bell & Beckwith, 114 E. Sandusky St. . . . I presented to Mr. Phillips my identification and a copy of the court order of Feb. 10. At my request, Mr. Phillips opened the office and installed new locks on both the front and rear entrance.
>
> The office is one-half of a small store front. Barney's Barber Shop occupies the other one-half of the store front. There are three rooms to the office, a small "conference" room, a long narrow rear storage room, and the main front room. The conference room was empty. The storage room contained miscellaneous supplies, trash, etc., of no apparent great value. The front room was furnished with two desks, two library tables, one wire service quotation machine, and several chairs (approximately 5 or 6). Thursday's [February 10] newspaper and mail was in the office and Friday's mail was delivered while I was present. The barber next door stated that the office had been closed all week and that he had accepted the mail and placed it in the office. The barber had a key to the Bell & Beckwith office as the storage room and utility controls are common to the barber shop and Bell

& Beckwith but are accessible only through the Bell & Beckwith office.

The landlord for the office is Champion Enterprises. The landlord's agent . . . was unable to provide a copy of the lease on Friday, but she said she would attempt to obtain one. . . . Both the barber shop and Bell & Beckwith share common utilities, and [the agent] stated that utility service would be continued. The common utility arrangement does present a problem in that the thermostat for the barber shop and Bell & Beckwith's office is located in the Bell & Beckwith office. I assured the barber and Mrs. Erhnswender [the agent] that we would provide them with keys to the Bell & Beckwith office as soon as possible.

While in Findlay, I visited banks and savings and loans within walking distance of the Bell & Beckwith office and inquired as to Bell & Beckwith's safe deposit boxes. No bank or savings and loan had record of a Bell & Beckwith box. I also visited the post office and had all mail stopped as of February 11.

At the Lima branch, Joseph Gregg found the ticker tape still on and the machine out of paper. He also found that the office had no mail delivery except at a post office box, and, at first, he couldn't find anyone with the authority to turn the mail over to him.

While the accountants were trying to make sense of Bell & Beckwith's bookkeeping systems (without any help, at that point, from the firm's employees, who were barred from the downtown building) and while other attorneys were taking care of security problems, McGraw was turning his attention to another pressing matter: discovering the rest of Ted Wolfram's assets.

He and a team of Fuller & Henry's lawyers had gone over Wolfram's hastily drawn list of assets that had been filed earlier in the week at the Lucas County recorder's office. Using that as a rough checklist, the team of lawyers interviewed Wolfram at length on February 11 at his home in Grand Rapids. Wolfram was not charged with anything at that point, and he wasn't under oath, but McGraw's theory was that he might be willing to talk more freely then than later.

The Fuller & Henry lawyers also got from Wolfram boxes of personal papers that had filled several cabinets in his sunken living room. The station wagon the lawyers drove to Grand Rapids wasn't big enough to haul away Wolfram's records—they had to rent a truck.

By February 16, Wolfram had made a handwritten list of his and his wife's interests in land, buildings, corporations, livestock, racehorses, planes, cars, and other properties and the estimated value of the interests. The list covered six pages of notebook paper and, in some cases, offered alternative property values. For example, it showed a quick-sale value of $25 million for the Landmark Hotel and Casino, encumbered by a $10 million mortgage and $5.2 million owed to Passport Travel on the land if it were sold. But Wolfram's list went on to show that merging the hotel property with another Wolfram entity, Mark III Corp., could produce a tax-loss benefit of $14 million. And he valued his eight Italian OSCA automobiles at "$800,000—subject to taking your time—$400,000 crash sale."

Disposing of some of the assets was relatively simple. Once an appraisal was made, a quick sale could be arranged. A Beechcraft King airplane was appraised at $315,000, but the trustee actually got $325,000 for it after Wolfram's pilot, Paul Goldsmith, offered to pay $10,000 over the appraised price. Another airplane, a Cessna Citation II jet, simply went back to the manufacturer because the highest appraisal was $1.9 million and Wolfram owed just over $2 million on the sales contract.

However, many of the Wolfram properties were difficult to sell because they could be offered only to a limited market. The Italian race cars, even though Wolfram's caveat about "taking time" to sell them was observed, went for far less than his estimates. A year and a half after the Bell & Beckwith bankruptcy case began, the trustee was still trying to find a collector to buy the last of them. One went for as little as $6,500. Still other properties were tied up in a tangle of partnerships, agreements, mortgages, notes, and similar encumbrances.

Some months into the case, McGraw decided that much of the Wolframs' property would have to be sold at auction. He even decided that the Wolframs' home on the Maumee River—impressing many visitors as more of a hunting lodge than a house—would bring a better price if sold at auction.

McGraw put together an amazing collection of property to sell at the first of the auctions, in December 1983, ten months after the brokerage collapsed. Some of the items, including a large picture that had adorned Wolfram's office wall, were too personal to sell and were returned to the Wolframs. The picture, labeled *Filly of the Year*, showed Zula Wolfram sitting on a hobby horse. (One of Zula's standardbred horses had been named the Ohio filly of the year.)

At the auction, held in a suburban motel, McGraw had a run-in with television crews. He had allowed a newspaper photographer to take pictures of some of the Wolfram property at a preview, but he wouldn't let TV crews shoot the actual bidding. One of the stations threatened to sue. The crowd included many curiosity seekers, but more than 100 registered to bid on the 106 items— mostly jewelry, furs, and household goods.

The auction started off slowly. A pottery falcon (the bird was the mascot of Wolfram's alma mater, Bowling Green State University) went for $20, a white-horse-on-velvet painting for $25, a pair of brass peacocks for $170. One diamond ring got $10,000 (the spectators, some of whom had been Bell & Beckwith customers, applauded) but several others went unsold. One of the more valuable pieces, a wildlife painting, was withdrawn after the auctioneer announced that bidding would start at the artist's offer of $10,000 and none in the crowd bid. Wolfram's stereo went for $35, and a man paid $85 for a silver-and-gold belt buckle and money clip monogrammed to imitate Wolfram's handwriting. By the end of the day, $53,000 was raised for the Bell & Beckwith estate.

But the hard part remained, and one of the hardest of the assets to sell was the Landmark Hotel, the money trap that had drained Wolfram of $15 million and led to his demise.

Above: The Landmark Hotel and Casino in Las Vegas had been bad luck for its previous owners, including Howard Hughes, but the luck was especially bad for Ted Wolfram—$15 million dollars' worth of bad luck.

Below: Wolfram, in a tweed sports coat, leaves the U.S. Court and Customs House after pleading guilty; in a dark coat is Frank McManus, his lifelong friend and attorney. In trench-coats are FBI agents.

I Debt   53,841,584 — EW ~ZW
                                             ~~57,200,000~~

Cash   5,800,000 — 4,904,348 —
Stock   5,000,000 — 5,805,655 —
Capital   ~4,000,000~ — 4,000,000 —
A/R B+Bjohns 600,000 =   600,000 — 13,307,003 —
            ~~15,000,000~~ —
            $38,155,000 TOTAL   37,539,581

〜〜〜〜〜〜〜〜〜〜〜

I Landmark —
   Land — Zula, Passport, Garg   18.7% 45%
   Mark III — Operating Co — Zula (81%), ~Garg~
   T2 Enterprise — non gaming. —
   Corporation owes Zula $4,500,000

If deed out, or Mark III assigned, hotel
is immediately closed —

Must merge to get full value.

Quick sale — $25,000,000 for bldg + land,
owe chimms $10,000,000 + $5,200,000 —

If Mark III merges, $14,000,000 in tax loss,
and has a value.

Passport owed $5,200,000 on land if sold.

Value — 10,000,000 on sale of land + bldg
        14,000,000 on merger of Mark III

W. Truax
JWA   Exhibit A

Part of the long list of assets Wolfram prepared in his own
handwriting after the brokerage collapsed.

Above: A pair of brass peacocks went for $170 at an auction of the Wolfram family's personal goods. At one time, live peacocks roamed the front and side lawns of their home.

Below: Auction in progress at Wolfram's home in Grand Rapids, Ohio. The home is a Frank Lloyd Wright derivative. It was valued at more than $300,000, but sold for $180,000.

Above: U.S. District Court Judge Nicholas Walinski leaves Toledo's Municipal Court after being sentenced to three days in jail for drunk driving.

Below: Patrick Foley prosecuted Wolfram on five counts that carried a maximum sentence of 25 years in prison.

Above: Patrick McGraw, the trustee for the liquidation of the 85-year-old Bell & Beckwith brokerage, administered a case that cost $3.2 million in legal fees and $2.8 million in accounting fees.

Below: William Connelly led the defense for Wolfram. His courtroom drama, though intriguing to spectators, didn't deter Judge Walinski from throwing the book at Wolfram.

Ted and Zula Wolfram leave the U.S. Court and Customs House after he was sentenced to 25 years in prison for his $47 million fraud. With them is their daughter-in-law Mrs. Edward Wolfram III, carrying their grandchild. In the background is Kevin Joyce, who assisted in the defense.

A passerby peers at the bankruptcy notice posted on Bell &
Beckwith's downtown Toledo office shortly after the firm was
closed by a court order.

Even though the brokerage building was still occupied by platoons of accountants, the sign on the building's facade suffers from neglect and vandalism.

© Las Vegas Review–Journal. All other photos reprinted by permission of the Toledo *Blade*.

7

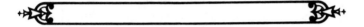

The $15 Million
Money Trap

The Landmark Hotel was haunted by the ghost of Howard
Hughes. And it was haunted by its image as an albatross.

The 30-story needle-nosed hotel with a distinctive
bulge at the top had taken nine years to build. It was
financed with tainted money, and the original developer,
Frank Caroll, had to sell it even before it opened. It was
bad luck for every owner afterward—particularly for Ted
and Zula Wolfram, since it siphoned off at least $15 million
of the money Wolfram diverted from the customers of Bell
& Beckwith.

One reporter called the Landmark "Frank Caroll's
folly, then Howard Hughes' headache, and Edward Wolfram's Waterloo." But one thing that kept the investors
coming, and still does, is the potential of the property:
Even though it is a long city block off the famed Strip, it is
across Paradise Boulevard from the huge Las Vegas con-
vention center, which could be its ultimate salvation. And
the Landmark has a colorful history. Over the years its
headliners have included Jimmy Durante, Dinah Shore,
Rich Little, Red Skelton, Connie Francis, Red Buttons,

Peggy Lee, Bob Newhart, the Oak Ridge Boys, and Buck Owens.

Although the unusual design of the Landmark has often been attributed to the Seattle Space Needle (built for the Seattle World's Fair), the design of the Landmark preceded the Space Needle by several years. Rough plans for the hotel began in 1957, when Frank Caroll, a Kansas City builder, first got the idea to build in Las Vegas. The name he chose was inspired by the Hollywood Landmark Motel, where he had stayed while taking the California contractors' examination.

Caroll began by building apartments and a shopping center, but by 1959 he had made final a plan for a 14-story hotel tower (later amended to allow for a 30-story tower so that the 327-foot height would make it Nevada's tallest building, taller even than the Mint Hotel, which rose at about the same time).

Caroll and his partners got a $3.3 million loan from the Appliance Buyers Credit Corp. in 1960 and began construction in late 1961.

Construction of the structure, with its cantilevered dome tied into the main shaft, was plagued from the start. One of the architects quit in the middle of construction, and about a year after construction began, the credit corporation backed out. The empty shell of the hotel lay dormant until 1966, when Caroll (who also goes by the name Frank Caracciolo) went to Kansas City to meet with Teamsters union officials and the late Nick Civella, who was at that time reputed to be the organized crime chief in Kansas City.

Caroll's Plaza Tower Co. came away from Kansas City with $5.5 million in financing from the Teamsters' Central States Pension Fund, and he obtained another $2.6 million the next year.

But by 1968, when the hotel was nearing completion, Caroll and his partners—his wife, Sue, Kansas City lawyer Sheldon Sandler, and California builder Louis Scherer—were besieged by creditors and, worse, were encountering difficulties with Nevada's gaming board.

In October 1968 the pension fund began foreclosure proceedings, but Robert Maheu, representing Howard Hughes, stepped in to offer $17.3 million for the unopened hotel and casino. Hughes had already been turned down by the Justice Department on his bid to buy the Stardust. Justice officials objected to the purchase on grounds that Hughes already owned the Sands, the Desert Inn, the Silver Slipper, the Castaways, and the Frontier. But in April 1969—possibly because of the enticement of the 1,100 jobs the 498-room hotel would provide—the Nevada Gaming Commission approved the transfer. The Hughes organization sent its last check to close the deal just before midnight on July 1, 1969, and the hotel opened the next day with a black-tie affair headlined by Danny Thomas.

The new hotel and casino seemed to offer great promise—it had a 250-seat nightclub, two top-line restaurants, 26 gaming tables, and more than 400 slot machines.

When the Wolframs bought the hotel in 1978, the *Blade* reported that the purchase evolved from a discussion (apropos of Wolfram's interest in sports) about basketball with Gary Yelverton—then an employee of Howard Hughes' Summa Corp. but later a part owner of the hotel during Wolfram's control.

Some details of the purchase come from a 1979 book, *The Sharing Society*, by Toledo industrialist Edward Lamb, who controlled the Nevada National Bank for a time:

> I like to recall a recent visit to my office by a young man who was a securities broker. He felt that he was working in a

dying business, and he wanted advice. I asked him what he wanted to do, and his answer was simply, "Make money, a lot of money."

I asked him if he had ever visited Reno and looked into the opportunities there. His reply was that his father had gone to Las Vegas as a tourist, but that he knew nothing else about the state. I told Paul Wolfram [a brother of Ted Wolfram who was also a broker at Bell & Beckwith] that practically any deal in the United States could be put together if one has guts and a million dollars. Wolfram replied, "I have a sister-in-law, Zula, with those qualifications." He was correct. Besides her beauty, imagination, and courage, she had a million dollars in U.S. Treasury notes resting quietly in the Toledo Trust Company.

Wolfram saw for-sale signs on property in Las Vegas next to the Hilton International Hotel. Upon inquiry, he found the price for the four-acre parcel: six million dollars. He returned to my office and reported his discovery. I asked him why he would want to buy raw land and build a hotel-casino, since he had no experience whatever in that line of business. I also told him the Howard Hughes estate's company, Summa Corporation, was eager to sell its Landmark Hotel. On his return to Toledo, he secured a partner or two to look into the matter. After tight negotiations, my young friends Paul and Ted Wolfram, with their associates, made a tender offer of $12.5 million for the project. Shortly thereafter their offer was accepted and they moved into Las Vegas to operate their new enterprise.

They sought a casino license, and the usual thorough investigation by the Nevada Gaming Commission took several months before granting permission to operate the casino. The occupancy of the hotel was even then running in excess of ninety percent. The hotel under Howard Hughes's management had lost million of dollars. The losses were due to poor management, skimmed-off gambling funds, and kickbacks in the various purchasing and trading departments. Summa Corporation levied a weekly management fee of thousands of dollars against each of its operating hotels. The total losses in the previous ten years amounted to more than fifteen million dollars. Many persons scoffed at the Wolframs' buying what they called "the worst dog in the Hughes kennel." The buyers moved in April 1978 and made some obvious changes, and within a couple of months, they had purchase offers of twenty-five million dollars!

How was this operation financed? Other than Zula's bonds, there were assets involved in the down payment, but one and a half million dollars was borrowed from my bank. Thus they put in a total of two and a half million dollars and had eight years to pay off the balance of the purchase price. In ten months of operation in the first year they claimed a net income before taxes of one million dollars. This profit resulted from their actual cash investment of only one million dollars!

What Lamb didn't know then was that Wolfram had bought the hotel with money that he didn't have. The $1 million Treasury security in Toledo Trust belonged to Bell & Beckwith, and the other $250,000 was illegally transferred to Nevada National Bank from a Bell & Beckwith account.

Wolfram often talked of expanding the hotel, by building a tower far bigger than the original 498-room structure and tying it into the original building to create a 2,300-room monstrosity.

Although the Wolframs lived in a $250,000 condominium near the Landmark, they also had offices in the hotel, and Zula ran her show-production operation there and spent considerably more time in Las Vegas than did Ted Wolfram.

Wolfram and his fellow investors borrowed $600,000 from Nevada National to use as operating funds to make payrolls and other expenses, but in the five years they operated the hotel-casino, were able to repay only half of it. The Landmark was caught up in the long recession that nearly destroyed many Las Vegas hotels, and it probably suffered more than most because of its gradually deteriorating condition. It never made money while Wolfram owned it, and in fact, the hotel owners weren't even able to meet their $133,000-a-month mortgage payments to Summa Corp.

Less than two years after buying the hotel-casino,

Wolfram was ready to sell off part of it for cash. When Bernard Glannon's Kansas City–based Passport Travel, Inc. went public in 1980, $4.5 million of the proceeds went to buy 18.7 percent of the Landmark's land, buildings, and property from the nominal owners at that time, Zula Wolfram and Gary and Sandy Yelverton. (Some other minority owners had been bought out earlier.)

The prospectus for Passport revealed a complicated financial arrangement. Mark III partnership, of which Zula Wolfram was majority owner, held title to the physical property of the Landmark but operated it under a lease agreement with Mark III Corp. (owned by basically the same group), and yet another company, F.A.M. Corp. (a wholly owned subsidiary of Mark III Corp.), operated the casino.

The arrangement with Passport also was complicated—requiring the payment of $1.50 a day per rented room to Passport, including rooms in any future expansions of the hotel. The prospectus placed the value of the hotel at $22 million, not including gambling equipment. And it noted that architectural renderings had been prepared for a hotel expansion and that construction financing was being negotiated.

Perhaps Wolfram should have believed more of what was in the prospectus than just the valuation. The prospectus noted a cumulative retained-earnings loss of $8 million and a Mark III Corp. operating loss of $1.6 million in the short time Mark III had operated it. "The hotel has historically operated at a loss," the prospectus said. And it pointed out that the occupancy rate was only 78 percent. It went on to discuss the extremely competitive nature of the Las Vegas hotel business and the potentially damaging effect of such factors as California fuel shortages.

Although the prospectus didn't mention Zula Wolfram's show productions, those were another source of financial trouble for the Landmark. The Landmark had its successes over the years, but it had some flops, too. One show in particular, called "Spellcaster"—the last show produced at the hotel—appeared to be losing $75,000 to $100,000 a month. It had a cast of 20 backing up the headliner, singer Roy Clayborne, whose act featured rock, country, and a bit of classical music. Clayborne was paid $2,000 a week, and his cast members' salaries varied from $300 to $500 a week apiece for the show in the hotel's Empire Room. The show was closed on short notice, the same weekend that the federal court order closed Bell & Beckwith. (The entertainers later sued for $408,000 in lost wages as a result of the unexpected closing.)

All this aside, the public offering did raise the $4.5 million, and Ted Wolfram proudly showed a $3 million check around Bell & Beckwith. And after that coup, who could question his ability as a wheeler-dealer and a financial wizard? At least until the collapse in early 1983.

A federal bankruptcy court hearing on September 14, 1983, to consider the sale of the Landmark to William Morris yielded nearly four hours of testimony about the hotel's operation. During the hearing, Richard Popeney, a partner with Ernst & Whinney, the trustee's accountants, said that, typically, an authorized clerk of Bell & Beckwith would call a bank to request a transfer of funds. He showed records indicating the transfer of nearly $15.4 million from Bell & Beckwith to accounts in Las Vegas from February 1978 to January 1983.

All told, Popeney said, 66 transfers occurred in that period—at least one a month, sometimes two or three a month. The disbursements ranged from $1,190 to $1,012,000, and the methods of transfer included wire and checks, mostly from two Toledo banks—Toledo Trust Co. and Ohio Citizens Bank.

The primary collateral, Popeney noted, was the

stock of Toto Ltd. Here's a portion of the court testimony (the questioner is Thomas Zaremba of Fuller & Henry):

Q: And why is that the primary source of collateral?

A: Because they're—over the period of these transfers, Toto, Limited, became the predominant value for those four accounts. . . .

Q: You indicated that exhibit 7 was a margin analysis maintained at Bell & Beckwith as of February 7th or 8th, 1978; is that correct?

A: That is correct. . . .

Q: From exhibit Number 7, can you determine what value was assigned to Toto, Limited, on the books and records of Bell & Beckwith as of that time period?

A: It lists the price at $375 per share for Toto, Limited.

Q: And exhibit 8, what does that report?

A: The quotation for Toto, Limited, stock on the foreign market in yen and converted, using . . . [the] exchange rates that are indicated for the 8th of February, the market price at that time, according to *The Wall Street Journal*, was $2.19.

Q: Did the value of Toto as quoted in *The Wall Street Journal* differ from the value as it was carried on the books and records of Bell & Beckwith?

A: Two dollars versus three hundred and seventy-five dollars.

Q: That is per share.

A: Per share.

Q: Just quickly, if you have performed that calculation, what is the total amount of the difference?

A: The difference times the number of shares in the columns comes to $635,000, approximately, rounded, taking the number of shares in the account times the difference between the $375 and the $2. . . .

Q: *The Wall Street Journal*'s quotations through February of 1983, as taken from the previous exhibits, indicate that Toto might have been worth $2 a share; is that right?

A: Rounded, that's correct.

Q: From the two documents that have been marked as exhibits 10 and 11, can you determine at what price or value Bell & Beckwith's books and records carried Toto as of February of 1983?

A: Those two exhibits listed the price at $99,999 [per share].

Q: And what is the total value of Toto carried on Bell & Beckwith's books and records?

A: 995 shares at $99,999 was 99 million, approximately $99,500,000.

Q: And how did that value compare with the value of Toto as priced in *The Wall Street Journal?*

A: It would be $1,661.

Popeney went on to say that the transfers were financed from customer deposit accounts or customer credits at Bell & Beckwith. Then, after the introduction of a number of additional exhibits—balance sheets, partnership assets, accounts receivable and payable—Popeney summarized the evidence:

A: The significance of those documents . . . [is] that they indicate that Bell & Beckwith had customer deposit accounts or customer credits of $54 million and it also indicates that they had partnership capital of about $5 million and they had some small borrowings of about $700,000. We know from the analysis of these accounts that they had made unsecured loans to those accounts of $25,800,000, so it's apparent in looking at these documents that they couldn't have financed the $25 million with the $700,000 bank borrowing or with the $5 million worth of capital, but with the $54 million of customer deposits or customer credit balances, so the significance is that it shows that the $25,800,000 in those accounts which included these transfers to Las Vegas were financed with customer credit balances and customer accounts. . . .

At a later point in the hearing, another Fuller & Henry attorney, Ray Farris, was questioning John VanRhyn, then controller and chief executive officer of the Landmark Hotel. It was established that the hotel received $13.8 million in cash infusions from Bell & Beckwith. The difference was explained by a $250,000 transfer that didn't show up on the hotel's books, a $1 million transfer that went directly to a bank, and another $750,000 that went to Lou and Jo Ann Tickel, who were co-buyers of the hotel. (Tickel was a former judge who also owned Ramada Inn franchises.)

Q: Do you have any knowledge, factual information or belief that leads you to think that the moneys that came from Bell & Beckwith infused into the Landmark were then siphoned off by either Mr. or Mrs. Wolfram?

A: I would have to say no, because [of] the fact . . . [that] the moneys that were sent in pretty much equal the amount of losses that were incurred over the years. There's no way that the Landmark could have continued to operate if moneys were diverted for another purpose other than covering the operating losses. . . .

Q: What do those figures show for the operating losses for the years that the Wolframs owned the Landmark?

A: For those years, approximately thirteen million, two. For the year of 1977 under Summa [Howard Hughes' operation], it was $5,675,000. . . . February through July [1983], we've incurred a profit of $206,000 and [in] August, the results just came in before my trip here and we had a loss of $186,000 for August of '83. . . .

Q: Would the Landmark have continued to operate without those cash infusions from Bell & Beckwith?

A: Under no circumstances.

For a time after the collapse of Bell & Beckwith, the trustee, in effect, operated the hotel. And now its new owner, William Morris, is trying to do what no one else has done: make the Landmark profitable.

Howard Hughes survived the Landmark to die of other causes; Ted Wolfram remains alive, but the Landmark killed his dream.

8

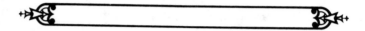

Friend Versus Friend

Although the civil side of the complicated Bell & Beckwith case moved swiftly, the criminal investigation proceeded at a deliberate pace. A month and a half after the collapse of the brokerage, there was still no hint of an indictment, and the press and public were getting restless.

The *Blade* received a barrage of letters from irate investors who wanted Wolfram brought to justice quickly. One reader from the small town of Lyons, Ohio, wrote:

> . . . The Wolframs' gluttonous appetite for things superseded business ethics and partners', customers' and bankers' trust. People that steal $36 million from 7,500 customers are not compassionate and generous. They are greedy and lecherous. . . . Our courts will have a test of justice. The tokens the Wolframs distributed to good causes and to people in high places . . . [are] not a balm for their deeds. Ohio's prisons and jails would be echo chambers if all persons were released that had committed lesser crimes than those crimes of the Wolframs.

A Toledoan wrote:

> . . . The Wolframs aren't such fancy people. As a matter of fact, she and he put me in mind of a couple of rats in a garbage can. Jesse James was a thief of the worst sort. These two

degenerates don't even have his manners. They stole money from people by the evil powers of their brain.

And a man from Waterville, a few miles away from Wolfram's home in Grand Rapids, wrote:

> . . . Why not tell the public that this was a near financial disaster for Toledo—and especially for more than 7,000—and I happen to be one who will be paying through the nose for many, many months to come. And the 7,000 multiply by two, and add a few children in, and you begin to see how many pockets these people had their hands in. Why not relate all the facts to the people of Toledo rather than trying to [make them] Saints Edward and Zula; now we have two new ones . . . ? Hold the bathroom door open. I've gotta heave.

The newspaper carried daily stories on the progress of the case, but about six weeks after the collapse of the brokerage, the paper began questioning the criminal-justice processes in its editorials. An editorial on March 20 entitled "$41 Million Questions" said in part: "The doors to Bell & Beckwith were clamped shut six weeks ago, and the case will not even be taken to a grand jury until April 5. Why has no one yet been charged or taken into custody or indicted in what is expected to be the largest single instance of individual fraud in the history of the federal Securities Investor Protection Corp.?" The same editorial also demanded to know: "Why were these soaring shortages in margin accounts that reached into the tens of millions of dollars over a period of five years or more never detected in periodic audits of the firm's records?" And: "Are there plans, as has been rumored, to plea-bargain on any possible charges to get them reduced to something of lesser severity?"

The truth is, plea bargaining *was* going on. For weeks, while the FBI and the SEC were investigating the case and while the district attorney's office was preparing the indictment, Wolfram was cooperating with the authorities—answering their questions about assets and the brokerage's tangled accounts. A conference room was set up on the second floor of the brokerage building, and Wolfram frequently came in to Bell & Beckwith to meet with the investigators. He and his attorneys also were trying to bargain for reduced charges.

Even though Wolfram could have been charged with any number of crimes, when the indictment finally came down from the grand jury, on April 5, 1983, it contained only five counts—four counts of fraud and one of falsification of documents. The indictment reiterated the charges that were already familiar to the public: that Wolfram had used the mails and wires to transfer most of the $32 million he had borrowed from the brokerage; that he inflated collateral worth $3 million to a false value of $383 million; and that he falsified telegrams, letters, and statements.

The indictment also repeated the familiar litany of Wolfram's uses for the diverted money—airplanes, purchase and renovation of antique cars, donations, loans, gifts, cattle ranches, a horse farm, the operation of the Landmark Hotel and Casino, and personal expenses.

The indictment did contain some previously unreleased information about the distribution of the money Wolfram took from the firm. It mentioned 67 wire transfers to the Landmark totaling $14,332,499.22 over a five-year period; 76 transfers totaling $3,181,118 to the horse farm in Ocala, Florida; $1,721,172.23 transferred to the oil company in Baton Rouge, Louisiana, through 52 wires; and 61 transfers totaling $955,483.56 to the farms in Arkansas.

Three days later, on April 8, Wolfram was arraigned before Judge Nicholas Walinski, the same federal judge who had held the hearing at Toledo Express Airport that began the long Bell & Beckwith case. Wolfram stood before the judge in a crowded courtroom and quietly pleaded guilty to all five counts, each of which carried a penalty of up to five years in prison and a fine of $10,000. "Guilty, sir, to all charges," Wolfram said.

Wolfram's father, Edward, Sr., put up his Grand Rapids home, valued at $150,000, as bail for his son. The home sat next door to Ted Wolfram's much larger home on the banks of the Maumee River.

The fact that although he was charged with a $47 million fraud, Wolfram was free on bail—and no hard cash was involved in the bail—led to some speculation in the community that he might get off with no prison term or a light sentence.

But most of those who thought an overly light sentence was possible didn't know Judge Walinski. Although Walinski has a reputation for compassion, he also has an Old-World sense of values and a long history on the bench. And he has a typical Republican leaning against criminal defendants and civil plaintiffs. In a quarter-century as a judge, Walinski had seen all the minor (and some major) scams, and he had seen the misery that even small-scale fraud can cause.

A lifelong Toledoan, Walinski had been a Navy pilot in World War II (and went on to become a captain in the Navy reserve), and after the war he returned to Toledo to serve as assistant law director and police prosecutor for five years.

Walinski was first a municipal judge and then a common pleas (county) judge, both elected positions. He was a familiar, friendly face around the Lucas County courthouse and had no trouble getting reelected time and again.

His name was probably a help, in that much of Toledo's population is Eastern European, and in local politics names like Pietrykowski, Lewandowski, and Czar-cinski are as common as Smith, Jones, and Miller would be in some cities.

He was named a federal judge by Richard Nixon in 1970 at the relatively young age of 49. A *Blade* editorial said of him at the time: "He is well and favorably known throughout the whole community. A friendly man, warm and compassionate, he will be as human on a federal bench as he has been on local courts. Let no man, however, try to take advantage of him on that count. He is knowledgeable in the law and will enforce it firmly."

As judges go, Walinski is not a scholar and has more of a seat-of-the-pants approach to interpretation of the law—his decisions show more of an interest in what the law can achieve than in the letter of the law.

On the federal bench, Walinski was somewhat isolated from his earlier experience. He missed the old-time politics of Toledo and never really lost the feeling of constantly running for office. So he may have taken the editorial insinuations of the local media more seriously than most federal judges (historically, most of the northern Ohio federal judges, even those sitting in Toledo, have come out of Cleveland).

Walinski had his share of personal problems. Two deaths within days of each other hurt him badly. His 17-year-old son, Nicholas III, died in a motorcycle crash, and two weeks later his longtime friend Common Pleas Judge George Kiroff died.

Judge Walinski had occasional problems with alcohol. For a while, he stopped drinking altogether. (However, less than a year after the Bell & Beckwith collapse and about four months after sentencing Wolfram, Walinski was arrested for drunk driving after a minor accident and served three days in the Toledo workhouse. Then, soon after that, he was arrested yet a second time; as a result, he spent a month in a Minnesota rehabilitation center for alcoholics and lost his driver's license for five years.)

The assistant DA at the time of the Wolfram case was Patrick Foley, a friend of Wolfram's defense attorney, William Connelly, and the man who took over the top prosecutor's job in 1972, a month after Connelly resigned to go into private practice.

Much of Connelly's stint as federal prosecutor involved cases against organized sports gambling, prostitution, and government corruption. His biggest local case was shutting down two houses of prostitution that had operated near Toledo since World War II. But his biggest claim to fame in his three years as assistant DA was being called on special assignment to act as first assistant prosecutor in the famous Father Berrigan bombing case in 1971, when Connelly was 30.

Connelly, a Catholic and an active Republican campaigner (among other assignments, he took on the chairmanship for northwest Ohio for Nelson Rockefeller's presidential bid), was chosen to help prosecute the Reverend Philip Berrigan and six others accused of plotting to kidnap presidential adviser Henry Kissinger and to blow up heating tunnels in Washington. The conspiracy charges were dismissed after a hung jury failed to return a verdict.

When Connelly left government service for private practice, a newspaper story reported that ". . . he gave an emphatic 'no' to a query about acting as a defense attorney in criminal cases in the future. 'I don't want to take advantage of what I've learned here to work against the system.' "

For the most part, Connelly kept that promise. He was basically a plaintiff's attorney until the Wolfram case came along, but he was developing quite a reputation, too, for defense in some civil suits. Some thought he might be Toledo's best trial lawyer since the late "Silver Dollar" Dan

McCullough, a colorful defender of the underworld fringe. In some ways, Connelly was the closest thing Toledo had to a Percy Foreman or a Melvin Belli.

Assisting Connelly in the defense was his associate, Kevin Joyce, and Frank McManus, Wolfram's longtime friend. In the days just before and immediately after the Bell & Beckwith collapse, the Wolframs transferred nearly $600,000 in checks, stocks, and bonds to their attorneys for the defense fund they knew would be needed (the attorneys eventually returned about $250,000 to the trustee, keeping $150,000 for Connelly and $200,000 for McManus).

The Wolfram case brought old friends Connelly and Foley together, but as foes. And it brought two different styles to the courtroom. Connelly had a reputation for courtroom theatrics and playing to the jury's sense of drama. Connelly enjoyed the thrill of courtroom combat. And he seemed to be an ideal choice for Wolfram because his reputation wasn't tainted by a history of criminal defense.

Prosecutor Foley could best be described as coming from the "I am sincere" school of trial lawyers. He reeks of sincerity when he tries a case, and in his 11 years as assistant DA leading up to the Wolfram case, he hadn't even the trace of a blot on his record.

While the prosecution and the defense were gearing up for the Wolfram hearing, a number of things were going on behind the scenes, including almost daily meetings between Wolfram and the federal authorities, who were trying to nail down all corners of the case. It took a long time to work out the details of the plea bargaining—an agreement that was later challenged, after the sentencing, by both Ted and Zula Wolfram.

In fact, the sentencing was taking entirely too long for many of the people in Toledo.

9

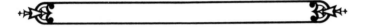

The Maximum

The date for sentencing Ted Wolfram had been postponed several times, and by the time the actual day arrived, September 6, 1983, there was great anticipation. An overflow crowd showed up at Toledo's federal courthouse in the civic mall, and television and newspaper photographers milled around the hallways of the old building hoping to get a glimpse of the Wolframs. Reporters for several newspapers in Ohio and Michigan, the Associated Press, *The New York Times*, and *The Wall Street Journal* shared the courtroom with investors big and small, a few former Bell & Beckwith employees, and a coterie of attorneys curious to see the drama that was certain to happen. It was the biggest case to be tried in Toledo in many a year.

Because Wolfram had pleaded guilty to all the charges in the indictment, the public was spared the expense of a long trial, but the fact-hungry press—and indirectly the public—was cheated out of the news opportunities a trial would have provided. There were many unanswered questions at the time: Exactly how did Wolfram divert the money from Bell & Beckwith to his other interests? Did he have accomplices? Were there even more assets hidden away?

The sentencing hearing, short as it was, did manage to answer some of the questions.

Among the 75 or so people who were able to get seats in the courtroom itself were three visitors from Chicago who had flown in just for the occasion. They were from the SEC, and they wanted to see their case through to completion. Joyce Lynch and Thomas Huber, two of the SEC attorneys who played large roles in the frantic effort to shut Bell & Beckwith down, joined their boss, William Goldsberry, at the sentencing.

Early in the 75-minute hearing, attorney William Connelly called his client, Wolfram, to the stand. Wolfram began by telling the court something that was not common knowledge at the time—that he had been stealing from Bell & Beckwith since about 1974. The indictment had only mentioned thefts since 1978. Wolfram's testimony also shows a man devastated by guilt and worried about the impact his crime and imprisonment would have on his family—his wife, his sons, even his five-year-old grandchild. The examination by Connelly went as follows:

Q: Did you over the past four or five or six years steal from Bell & Beckwith?

A: Yes, I did.

Q: Would you tell the court when you started and what you did?

A: I started sometime, approximately 1974 [it later turned out to be 1973], and by artificially inflating the value of one stock, Toto Limited, of Japan, and borrowing against those values, I systematically stole money from the customers of Bell & Beckwith.

Q: Anyone else involved in this scheme?

A: No sir.

Q: Under the terms of an agreement with the trustee for Bell & Beckwith you agreed and your wife agreed to turn over to the trustee all of your assets. What have you done in fulfillment of that agreement?

A: Turned over everything.

Q: What do you own now?

A: Some furniture and pots and pans, some personal clothing, my wedding band—my wife's wedding band and engagement ring went to the trustees. A minor amount of costume jewelry for my wife. Very little.

Q: Also as part of that plea agreement you agreed to submit to a polygraph examination. Did you in fact do so?

A: Yes sir.

Q: Who administered that polygraph examination?

A: The FBI.

Q: In the area of hidden assets were you specifically asked whether or not you have concealed assets or have assets in the possession of some third party who is holding them for your benefit or that of your wife? Were you asked that?

A: Yes.

Q: Did you answer?

A: Yes.

Q: What was your answer?

A: I do not.

Q: Did you pass a polygraph examination

A: Yes sir.

Q: Were you also asked during the course of that examination whether or not anyone was involved with you in this scheme?

A: Yes, I was.

Q: What did you indicate?

A: No one else in this world.

Q: Did you pass?

A: Yes sir.

Q: Did you ever for a moment think of the injury and harm you were causing to account holders at Bell & Beckwith with what you did?

A: I had no idea of the amount of damage and the amount of misery and uncomfort I was causing them, the worry, the anxiety. I had no idea what I was doing.

Q: I would like you to tell the court how it was during that period of time that you were involved in this scheme.

A: It is never a quiet moment in your life when you start something like this. I have always been an honest man. I have always been generous with my children and my family and friends, and to do something like this preyed on my mind terribly.

I tried several times to extricate myself, but the only thing I did was dig myself in deeper. But like all criminals I did not deserve to escape by working my way. I deserve what I am going to receive.

Q: When did you first tell your family? How did this first come about?

A: February 5th [before the federal court hearing at the airport] I called Frank McManus, attorney and long-time friend, and I called my family in the area and asked them to come to my home. They arrived at around 8 o'clock in the morning. I told them what I had done. I was an evil man, and I had very gravely damaged each of them and also the customers of Bell & Beckwith, and I had stolen a great deal of money.

Q: What impact has this had upon you and your family?

A: Well, the impact on me is deserved. Let's not discuss that my family has been suffering, although they're part of it.

How do I face my grandchildren? Every time I look at them, I cry. How do I tell a 5-year-old what I have done—of the terrible thing I have done to them, and particularly the boys named Wolfram. From now on that name is going to be a terrible name in this town.

I have a 17-year-old son. I have just a horrible time talking to him because I know that during the time he most needs me I am not, probably not, going to be available to give him aid and comfort.

But the person who suffered the most is my wife. She knew absolutely nothing about it. Through almost 29 years of marriage, she has been an absolute saint. I love her so much and I do this to her. The insincerity, the hypocritical insensitivity toward my family and myself is killing me. I can barely think of anything but what I have done to everyone, not only myself and my family. At night these monsters are four times as large, so sleep is impossible. That is what I deserve; what I did was wrong, and I am very, very unhappy about what I did.

Q: What would you say to any person in a financial institution or brokerage house who is about to take that first dollar?

A: They have no idea what they're creating. The monster they think they might create is nothing like the monster they will create. The way that they will destroy everybody and finally themselves, they'll never know from that moment on what they might have done if they had done things honestly. I would say come and talk to me for five seconds and you will not follow my act.

Q: Is there any other statement that you would care to make to the court?

A: Just that I am terribly sorry that everyone has to be here. I am doing this to myself. The judge and the fine people that are surrounding me have done nothing to me. I am doing it to myself. I love this area of the country, and I have been one of the biggest backers of the area. If it is ever over, I won't be able to walk the streets, free to walk the streets and say I am terribly embarrassed and ashamed and hate myself, and I don't think in my lifetime I will ever get over this.

Prosecutor Foley asked only three brief questions:

Q: You indicated at the time of the fraud, from '74 until it ended in February of this year, you didn't realize the enormity of the fraud. Is that right?
A: Yes sir.
Q: You are now aware, sir, that that was the largest [individual broker] fraud in nearly fifty years of the Securities and Exchange Commission?
A: Yes.
Q: You have indicated you have always been generous with friends. You now acknowledge your generosity was from other people's money?
A: Yes sir, from the time this started.

Connelly, however, was undaunted by Foley's remarks and went on to paint a picture of Wolfram as a sincerely compassionate man. He referred to a letter written by Monsignor Jerome Schmit saying that in his experience, covering 30 years at St. Patrick's Church in Toledo, there were "constantly poor people whom Mr. Wolfram helped, and Mr. Wolfram helped many young people with college tuition."

The only witness who took the stand, other than Wolfram himself, was football coach Don Nehlen, who was then at West Virginia University but who had coached at Bowling Green for 12 years.

Q: Would you describe to the court your relationship and your wife's relationship with the Wolframs?
A: Well, Ted and Zula and Mary Ann and I

probably from '65 until I left Bowling Green were probably two of our very best friends, closest friends. We used to spend time with them socially. He helped me a lot on my job at Bowling Green, and, you know, I just think the guy is a super guy. And I think he made a mistake, but I don't think he is a criminal, and that is why I am here.

Q: How often did you see the Wolframs?

A: Oh, I probably talked to Ted three, four times a week, and when we'd lose, he'd come around, and when we'd win he wouldn't come around. So he probably came around more than I would have liked. . . . We'd go to their home maybe two, three times a month. I don't know exactly how many times we'd go up there. Wherever you go in Ted and Zula's home, Zula would have cowboy boots and Levi's on, and . . . you weren't there very long before she had her shoes off, and you'd have your shoes off . . . and, you know, just typical family.

Q: What do you believe, knowing him as you do, knowing his family, would be an appropriate punishment?

A: . . . The only thing I know about Ted . . . in my opinion, when my football players make a mistake we try to help them out. I don't think Ted Wolfram is a bad person. He made a terrible error, and he admitted it.

Connelly, well known as a somewhat theatrical lawyer, delivered a dramatic closing argument:

> . . . And finally, what of Ted Wolfram? Thursday, he will be 54 [actually a misstatement; Wolfram was two days short of his fifty-third birthday]. Wherever you send him he is going to have time to think. And he will have time as he sits wherever he is to think about what he has done to his children, to his parents, to his wife, to his brothers, all of whom have a name to be ashamed of. He can think that after 54 years he is going to leave his wife and his oldest son homeless [the oldest son, Edward III, nick-named Fritz, lived in a home owned by Wolfram]. He can think

that while he is sitting there that as they start out for Florida trying to build a new life that essentially Mrs. Wolfram has no marketable skill, and his son is but a senior in high school, and they take with them as the sum total of their property whatever is left them—three beds, three tables and two TVs.

[Actually, they kept a little more than that—a refrigerator, a portable microwave oven, living room chairs, washer and dryer, a large-screen video system, some miscellaneous furniture, and an old Mercedes.]

He can think of the impact that this has had on his family on the morning of February 4th [actually February 5] before anyone else began to publicly disclose what he had done—the impact upon them, that he told them he was a thief and the realization that he is. And the hurt and anger that it caused each of them. He can think that while he is in prison he is absolutely powerless to be of any assistance to his youngest son [Ian] and when last year in English class at St. John's High School the world "pilfer" came up and another kid said, "Hey, let Wolfram answer that one." So he will leave his son without much defense. Certainly no defense to the name Wolfram.

Connelly also made much of Wolfram's cooperation with the authorities. "Ted Wolfram's cooperation was the essence of the plea agreement," Connelly said. "Had he not [been cooperative] it would have been necessary to have five or six FBI agents specializing in accounting. But there was full cooperation. . . . That cooperation saved a lot of people."

Connelly said that Wolfram readily gave up his large home, collector cars, and personal property except for personal effects worth about $2,200. "Other than that, everything they have has been turned over to the trustee."

Connelly informed the court that the uninsured loss in Bell & Beckwith could eventually be reduced to $6.8 million, and he said he had reason to believe that the auditors' insurance might total more than $10 million in coverage. "The impact on our community is less severe than originally anticipated," he said. ". . . In terms of protecting society, Mr. Wolfram is not a threat."

He noted the 18-month prison terms served by Watergate conspirators John Mitchell, Robert Haldeman, and John Erlichmann, and he added that Judge John Sirica reduced the sentences from eight to four years for each defendant. "I believe he did so because he recognized that by their own action they destroyed their lives. . . . They all live in disgrace."

At the end of his somewhat impassioned argument, Connelly suggested to Judge Walinski that an appropriate sentence for Wolfram would be two years in prison and 1,000 hours of public-service work each year for three years.

Judge Walinski had in front of him a 33-page pre-sentencing report prepared largely by the federal parole authorities. The judge didn't reveal the full contents of the report (which included a great deal of personal information about the Wolframs, such as the deaths of four of their children shortly after their births), but he did read a portion of it. One portion was a letter from prosecutor Foley, which indicated that Wolfram's cooperation did save the government some months of investigation and that Wolfram passed a polygraph examination aimed at discovering whether he had hidden any assets from the government.

However, Foley's letter said that "as late as February [Wolfram] attempted to deceive the SEC" and began cooperating with the authorities "only after it was clear he was caught."

When Judge Walinski had heard both arguments and was ready to pronounce sentence, it started to become clear that his Old-World sense of decency was offended by Ted Wolfram's actions. Walinski began by saying that even the small investors had been damaged by Wolfram's diversion of money from the brokerage and that "some larger investors have been hurt beyond recall. . . . Almost everyone who was a customer of Bell & Beckwith has been hurt."

And, the judge said, "The fact that SIPC has covered most of the losses to date is no credit to Mr. Wolfram." He noted that SIPC's reserve fund was so depleted by the Bell & Beckwith case that SIPC had to raise its fees charged broker-dealers all over the country.

With Wolfram standing in front of him, Judge Walinski moved swiftly from his lecture into the sentencing. He told Wolfram that "this court is in a position that it has never been in in 25 years," and he said that what he was going to have to do to Wolfram's family was "personally distasteful."

Cynics had been saying that Wolfram would get off with probation or a very light prison sentence, but Judge Walinski quickly dispelled that notion. With no hesitation, he rattled off the sentence: "Five years on count 1. . . . Five years on count 2, consecutive with count 1. . . . Five years on count 3." And so on, until the entire 25-year sentence was levied.

"That's the maximum sentence I can impose," he told Wolfram, "and I'm sorry I have to do that. . . . I'm sorry I have to do this to you and your family. I consider them as much a victim as the customers of Bell & Beckwith."

Judge Walinski ordered Wolfram to surrender to a federal prison on September 30, and he said he would recommend to the federal Bureau of Prisons that Wolfram be allowed to serve his sentence at Eglin Air Force Base in Florida (considered to be the "country club" of prisons because of its light security and the preponderance of white collar criminals).

It turned out that neither of those things happened.

Wolfram was given until October 3 to turn himself in, as inmate No. 40643-060, to a medium-security prison, the Federal Correctional Institution in Tallahassee, Florida, a facility with barracks but no bars. The Bureau of Prisons opted for a Florida prison at least partly because Wolfram's wife and parents had said they would be moving to Florida.

After the sentencing, a pale, grim, and shaken Wolfram, his family, and attorneys took the long walk across the civic mall while the TV cameras ground away.

Some skeptics were surprised at the severity of the sentence, but Wolfram drew no sympathy from the local press. An editorial in the *Blade* several days later concluded:

> While Wolfram was systematically looting the firm he headed as managing director, he was living high and handsomely—private jet, a stable of race horses, cattle farms, a hotel in Las Vegas, a collection of antique cars, the works. It does not seem unjust that he spend a long, long time behind bars in a federal prison where the routine leaves plenty of time after prison work hours for Wolfram to contemplate the tribulations his lawlessness has brought to scores of others.

10

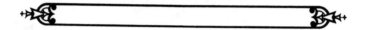

Searching for Blame

During the months before and after Ted Wolfram's sentencing, investigators for the SEC, the FBI, and the Ohio Division of Securities were trying to piece together the events that led to Wolfram's assuming, and abusing, his obvious power at Bell & Beckwith.

There was suspicion of collusion, secret deals, diversion of assets to favored customers just before the firm's demise. But in the final analysis, after conducting hundreds of hours of interviews (some partners and former partners were questioned for up to five hours at a time) and after poring over thousands of pages of records, the investigators found no other criminals to charge.

Investigators took depositions from nearly everyone in the firm and questioned such employees as margin clerks at great length—only to find them guilty of nothing more damaging than gullibility.

However, there was plenty of blame to spread around. Hundreds of millions of dollars worth of lawsuits have been filed against the auditors, the partners, the Wolframs, and the Bell & Beckwith estate. And the SEC has formally censured one auditing firm and placed strictures against Bell & Beckwith's former partners. For a time, the liquidation trustee also considered suing the New York Stock Exchange, the American Stock Exchange, and the National Association of Securities Dealers for failing to monitor Wolfram's accounts but decided not to.

About two weeks after the collapse of Bell & Beckwith, a class-action suit for $100 million was filed in Lucas County Common Pleas Court against Wolfram and the accounting firms of Frederick S. Todman & Co. of New York and Arthur Young & Co. The suit alleged that the accounting firms knew or should have known that balance sheets and audits did not give an accurate picture of the firm's financial condition. Arthur Young immediately responded that it had not been an auditor for Bell & Beckwith since the fiscal year ended March 31, 1976, seven years before it failed.

And two weeks after that suit was filed, the seven general partners other than Wolfram filed a $40 million suit in U.S. District Court against Todman and one of the accounting firm's partners, Victor M. Marchioni.

That suit contended that if proper audits had been made, the partners would have been alerted to the pattern of the misappropriation of assets by Wolfram, and it accused the accountants of not exercising ordinary care, skill, and diligence. It also claimed that the Bell & Beckwith partners had suffered damage to their business and to their reputations.

Bernard Weiner, senior partner of Todman, was quoted in the press as calling the suit "ludicrous" and he said that although the Todman auditors were in Toledo only once a year for the annual audit, the Bell & Beckwith partners were at the firm year-round and that they each signed quarterly reports to the New York Stock Exchange.

On April 29, 1983, nearly three months after the collapse, Patrick McGraw, the liquidation trustee, filed a $72 million suit against Todman in federal bankruptcy court in Toledo. That suit sought compensatory damages for losses of $47.5 million and punitive damages of $25 million. Since by that time Wolfram had been indicted for fraud, one of Todman's partners told the press that Wolfram had admitted his criminal acts and had deceived and lied to accountants. The unidentified partner said his firm was a victim of Wolfram's fraud.

McGraw's lawsuit against Todman, which has become a central issue in the bankruptcy of the brokerage, raised some new allegations:

> From at least April 1, 1976, through at least April 25, 1980, the system of internal control and system for safeguarding securities failed to provide adequate procedures, safeguards and security to prevent the fully paid and excess margin securities of a customer from being hypothecated without the express written consent of such customer. Said failures resulted in securities from the accounts of J. J. Schedel and Charles McKenny being unlawfully hypothecated by Wolfram. . . .
>
> From at least April 1, 1976, through Feb. 5, 1983, the system of internal control failed to require that a customer account be [in] the name of the true, beneficial owner unless a written statement signed by the true, beneficial owner attesting to his or her ownership of the account was obtained. Such failure enabled Wolfram to conceal his ownership of and proprietary interests in the Wolfram accounts.
>
> . . . The system of internal control did not require separate identification of accounts maintained for partners, employees, their relatives and entities in which they had a substantial interest, so that such accounts could be reviewed by an appropriate independent partner or employee and by examining authorities. . . .
>
> . . . The system of internal control did not provide for the periodical review of the margin accounts by a partner or employee with no duties in connection with such accounts, to determine that minimum margin requirements were being maintained. . . .
>
> . . . The system of internal control did not provide for the appropriate segregation of duties and rotation of personnel and

responsibilities in key areas. Such failures allowed Wolfram uninterrupted access to and control over both the assets of Bell & Beckwith (the Wolfram accounts and Wolfram receivables) and accounting records (the margin account records, customer account records, etc.) which he employed in conducting and concealing the Wolfram fraud.

. . . The system of internal control failed to require that prices used in computing margin requirements be obtained from independent, reliable sources. Such failure enabled Wolfram to use grossly inflated prices for the Toto shares in his scheme to obtain credit through the Wolfram accounts.

The filing by the trustee went on to allege several breaches of generally accepted accounting standards:

The examinations were not performed by persons with adequate technical training and proficiency as auditors. Most, if not all, of the assistants employed in the Bell & Beckwith examinations were not certified public accountants. Most lacked formal training in accounting and auditing. Most were not college graduates.

The work was not adequately planned and assistants were not adequately supervised. Planning meetings were seldom, if at all, held among those assigned to each examination prior to its commencement. Assistants were not regularly included in such meetings. Few, if any, written audit procedures were prepared for the guidance of the assistants. Assistants conducted the bulk of the 1981 audit without the day-to-day, on-site supervision of a senior auditor. Marchioni acted as the senior auditor for the 1981 audit while also acting as the senior auditor for a larger examination in Cleveland, Ohio. Marchioni visited Bell & Beckwith on no more than three occasions during the 1981 examination. Two of Marchioni's visits lasted no more than one day and the third no more than two days.

No proper study or evaluation of Bell & Beckwith's system of internal control was made. The study, if any, made by Todman consisted merely of discussing the system of internal control with Bell & Beckwith's personnel and management. No transactions were traced through the system to determine if it operated as described. Little, if any, documentation of the auditor's understanding of the system was prepared. No written evaluation of the system was made. The system was not documented by written narrative or graphic description. Few, if any, tests were made of transactions processed by the system during each audit period.

Sufficient competent evidential matter was not obtained, through inspection, observation, inquiry and confirmation. At least during the 1981 and 1982 examinations, Bell & Beckwith's margin accounts were examined by reviewing the margin account status report while the same was in the hands of Wolfram. This report carried no listing of prices for the securities held in the margin accounts and did not give the extended value of each security. The margin status report was "eyeballed" while Wolfram turned the pages. No effort was made to (1) trace the securities held in the accounts to the customer statements and stock records, (2) verify that the margin status run contained all margin accounts (for example, by "footing" the account balances and tieing the total to a general ledger account, (3) verify the market value and loan value of the securities held in the margin accounts, (4) determine that such securities had loan value under Regulation T. Prices used in computing market and loan values were "tested" by observing the margin clerk entering prices into the Bell & Beckwith electronic data processing system, but no attempt was made to verify that the prices entered were properly processed. No attempt was made to obtain independent verification of the prices entered. No review was made for unusual prices, for unusual market and loan values, for the unusual account balances, or for accounts in the names of partners, employees or related parties (i.e., known family members or entities in which partners, employees and known family members had substantial interests).

Todman did not communicate with Bell & Beckwith's predecessor auditor [Arthur Young] either before or after the initial acceptance of the engagement for the 1977 audit. Marchioni and Weiner were aware that the predecessor auditor had required that a notice of material deficiency of Bell & Beckwith's system of internal controls be reported to examining authorities during the 1976 examinations.

The suit by the trustee named as defendants the general partners of Todman, including Marchioni, Weiner,

Lester S. Cooper, George Zelin, and Irving B. Freedman. An amended version of the suit filed two months later named several other accountants as defendants: Andrew Epstein, Alan S. Koppel, Arnold Beiles, and Franklin Zuckerman. The amended complaint also alleged that some of Schedel's and McKenny's securities that were supposed to be in Bell & Beckwith's control had actually been pledged for bank borrowings and had been in the banks' control. And the amended suit scaled down the damages to amounts of "at least $40 million" compensatory and $25 million punitive.

More than a year after the original trustee's lawsuit, on July 9, 1984, the Todman defendants filed their answers and counterclaims, taking exception to all the trustee's claims. One part of the defendants' document said: "As an essential part of this scheme, Wolfram, who was designated by Bell & Beckwith and by its general partners as, and vested with the actual and apparent authority of, the managing partner of Bell & Beckwith, intentionally, willfully, wantonly, maliciously, recklessly and without regard to their truth or falsity, made false statements to Todman in response to inquiries made by Todman in the performance of its audits of Bell & Beckwith."

The statement went on to say that Todman, "after its own reasonable investigation, had reasonable grounds to rely on . . . these representations, assurances and certifications of Wolfram. . . ."

And it asserted, "The general partners of Bell & Beckwith aided and abetted the Wolfram fraud by acting in reckless disregard of Wolfram's activities at Bell & Beckwith and by recklessly failing to discover Wolfram's activities at Bell & Beckwith."

The Todman defendants' statement said the Bell & Beckwith partners "ratified" Wolfram's actions and "knew or should have known of Wolfram's fraudulent activities or should have discovered [them]."

In their counterclaim, the Todman defendants said, "Todman has been required to spend in excess of $300,000 complying with the investigatory requests of government agencies and defending numerous civil actions, including this action, and anticipates additional expenditures of at least $700,000." The counterclaim went on to suggest that Bell & Beckwith's partners should indemnify Todman against liability.

Even while pretrial motions were being heard in the trustee's case against Todman, the SEC took action against Todman, on August 20, 1984. The commission suspended Marchioni from practice for six months, saying that Todman and Marchioni failed to perform their audits with persons having sufficient training and proficiency and failed to adequately plan and supervise the audit staff or perform proper tests.

The SEC also cited "materially false and misleading" financial statements and said that Todman and Marchioni

> failed to disclose that the receivables from customers reflected as an asset on Bell & Beckwith's balance sheet consisted predominantly of Wolfram's debts to the firm which were collateralized by nearly worthless securities . . . thereby failing to disclose that Bell & Beckwith was insolvent. For example, in the audited financial statements of April 30, 1982, Bell & Beckwith reported as an asset customer receivables amounting to almost $45 million, the bulk of which were Wolfram's borrowings that were collateralized primarily by securities valued on Bell & Beckwith's books at over $87,000 a share but which were actually worth approximately $1.80 a share.

The SEC officially censured the Todman firm and ordered that Todman employ an outside reviewer to oversee its audit procedures; that the firm provide its partners and audit staff with 40 hours of outside professional training each year for two years; and that after serving his six-month suspension, Marchioni submit his audit work for outside review for another six months.

The SEC issued a four-page, single-spaced memorandum for use as a checklist by the outside reviewers.

On January 29, 1985, just days before the expiration of the two-year statute of limitations on civil suits involving the Bell & Beckwith bankruptcy, the liquidation trustee and Arthur Young & Co. made a surprise move—they reached an out-of-court settlement for Arthur Young to pay $388,512.44 in return for a release from any future claims.

Arthur Young denied any liability or wrongdoing, but the manager of the firm's Toledo office, Warren Buckey, signed the agreement, apparently to protect the firm against costly litigation.

Documents filed with the court showed that Ted Wolfram's accounts had a deficiency of $320,000 in the last year that Arthur Young audited Bell & Beckwith, but the deficiency didn't show up in the statements or opinions.

There were numerous objections to the out-of-court settlement—the main argument being that if Arthur Young had caught the Wolfram fraud in its early stages, the later, more costly frauds wouldn't have occurred and that Bell & Beckwith was technically insolvent as early as 1976, the last year Arthur Young audited the firm. Trustee McGraw and the lawyers from SIPC, however, argued that it would cost at least a million dollars to take Arthur Young to court and that there was no certainty of getting more than the agreed-to settlement of $388,512.44.

During the four-day hearing on the Arthur Young settlement, a document called the "Waterman memo" surfaced. The memo, written by an Arthur Young partner, John Waterman, in 1976, explained how Arthur Young lost the Bell & Beckwith auditing job to Todman. In the memo, Waterman said the Bell & Beckwith partners were disturbed about Arthur Young's insistence on issuing a "material deficiency" report with the 1976 audit—a report that pointed out the inadequacy of the posting system (mostly manual) and the rising error rate. And, according to the Waterman memo, Arthur Young was "fired" when it was underbid by Todman. Arthur Young's bid for the next audit was 1,400 to 1,500 hours at a total rate of $20,000 to $22,500 plus expenses, and Todman's bid was for $16,500 to $20,000.

And in the final days before the statute of limitations ran out, the bankruptcy judge, Richard Speer, allowed several additional suits to be filed against Todman—although it had been generally understood that the $65 million suit by the trustee against Todman would have precedence over all the other Todman suits.

Among the last-minute actions against Todman were a suit by Joseph Schedel's estate seeking $1.5 million in compensatory damages and $4.5 million in punitive damages, a suit by businessman Robert Hylant for $300,000 compensatory and $3 million punitive damages, and two suits by various members of the Wolfram family seeking indemnification for claims against the Wolframs and damages of $150,000 to $10 million. That last suit, filed by the Wolfram children, named as defendants both Todman and Arthur Young as well as the SEC, the New York Stock Exchange, the American Stock Exchange, and the National Association of Securities Dealers.

Late in January 1985, it was the Bell & Beckwith general partners' turn to take the blame for the debacle.

First, the SEC issued sanctions against Wolfram's seven partners, barring them from ownership of or supervisory roles with any brokerages or investment companies in the future. The administrative order said that the partners aided and abetted Bell & Beckwith's violations of the SEC's net-capital, customer-protection, and reporting rules.

It went on to say that six of the partners signed "materially inaccurate" documents such as the FOCUS report filed with the SEC (FOCUS is an acronym standing for the Financial and Operational Combined Uniform Single report), "which they had not read or reviewed and [so] had no basis for believing that the information . . . was accurate." And the order said that the seventh partner, Donald Henninger, "did not have sufficient training or qualifications to prepare them." Henninger, the last partner to buy in at Bell & Beckwith, late in 1980, later worked for a time for Oberweis Securities but left for FS Equities, a business brokerage in Houston.

Four of the other six were, at the time of the order, selling stocks and bonds for the Toledo branch of Cowen & Co.: J. Robert Jesionowski, George Todd, Robert R. Coon II, and John E. Thompson. (That branch has since closed.) Two were with Oberweis Securities in Toledo: Roscoe R. Betz and Thomas L. McGhee.

Jesionowski, on behalf of all the former general partners, issued a brief statement to the press, part of which read: "No individual partner other than Edward P. Wolfram, Jr., is guilty of any illegal conduct after thorough investigation by several investigatory bodies."

A few days after the SEC's administrative order, the partners were hit again—this time by McGraw, the liquidation trustee, who filed suit against them and five other former general partners, in federal court, literally just hours before the expiration of the statute of limitations. All told, McGraw filed 13 suits in one day, out of a total of 16 Bell & Beckwith suits filed that day.

The long-expected suit against the partners named as co-defendants Wolfram and the seven other general partners and five former partners who had sold out their interest at some point during the Wolfram years: Richard J. Foote (retired); Robert M. Fox, Jr. (then manager of

Cowen & Co.'s Toledo office); Louis Haubner, Jr. (with Prescott, Ball & Turben in Lima, Ohio); Grafton M. Mouen (with the Investment Management & Research division of Raymond, James & Associates); and James J. Secor, Jr. (with William C. Roney & Co.'s Toledo office).

Several of those named had long family associations with the old brokerage: Wolfram and Coon were second-generation brokers there; Secor was a grandson of one of the firm's founders; and Mouen's father had been a senior partner of the brokerage for many years.

The trustee's suit didn't name a specific damage amount but noted that the Ohio code made the general partners all liable, jointly and severally, for the full amount of the deficiency and the former general partners liable "to the extent provided by law."

McGraw also asked the court for the return of withdrawals some of the partners had made in the firm's last year of business, ranging from $59,000 for Coon to $283,000 for Betz and $10.8 million for Wolfram. And the suit asked for Betz to return $60,000 on a promissory note from Zula Wolfram and $200,000 on a loan from Ted Wolfram.

The trustee also suggested an unusual way to extract some of the money from the partners. The suit asked that the court order the partners to apply their share of the firm's $43 million loss in the year 1983 against their personal income tax—carried back to 1980 and forward to 1998.

After the barrage of last-minute lawsuits, all that remained of the case was winding down the long legal processes and learning some important lessons.

11

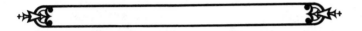

Just a Freak
Occurrence
or
Gamblers at Heart?

It's hard to imagine that $47 million could disappear without something tangible and constructive emerging from the whole sordid experience. Yet it seems almost nothing concrete came out of the Bell & Beckwith scandal or out of the several other brokerage frauds that occurred at about the same time. No new rules were written, and few, if any, procedures were changed.

There were, however, some lessons learned in the aftermath of the fraud, amorphous and late-arriving though they may have been.

To put those rather ephemeral lessons in perspective, it is helpful to review what really happened in the Bell & Beckwith case and in two similar but entirely unrelated frauds—the crash of Stix & Co. in St. Louis in late 1981 and the collapse of G. V. Lewellyn & Co., Inc. in Des Moines in March 1982.

All three frauds have uncanny common denominators. All involved brokers who were ambitious dreamers— and all three men were gamblers at heart, willing to risk everything to achieve the wealth and/or power their egos demanded. They also were gamblers in another sense. Each had a fascination with casinos, horse racing, or sports betting. And all three had expensive tastes in cars, houses, and baubles. They lived well and reached too far.

The three who brought their brokerages to ruin— Ted Wolfram, Thomas Brimberry, and Gary Lewellyn— invested heavily in other ventures. They spent a substantial part of what they stole on what could have been excellent investments if too many things hadn't gone wrong.

The three fraud-induced liquidations, occurring in just over a year's time, cost the Securities Investor Protection Corp. $71 million, of which about $8 million was recovered over a three-year period—and if the Federal Deposit Insurance Corp.'s losses are included (one of the brokerage failures also caused a bank failure), the three embezzlements cost nearly $90 million.

These three cases fit into a general pattern of increased brokerage losses in recent years. SIPC's five most expensive cases all came between 1981 and 1983, resulting in SIPC's fund dropping from a high of $219 million in 1981 to a low of $141 million—below its statutory floor of $150 million—in May 1983. (The depletion of funds caused SIPC to reimpose an assessment of 0.25 percent on broker-dealers' gross revenues.)

An indication of the severity of the three major frauds is found in the overall statistics since SIPC's founding. Since 1970, its *average* payout was just over $500,000 in 173 cases (excluding the five most expensive). The 173 cases, most of which did not involve fraud, cost a total of $88 million, while the five big ones required advances of $83 million, or roughly half of SIPC's total advances of $171 million.

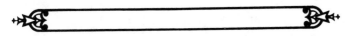

The first of the well-publicized cases was Stix & Co., a 69-year-old St. Louis firm, which broke into the news November 4, 1981, when the IRS and FBI simultaneously raided the firm and confiscated its records.

At the root of Stix's problem was Thomas Brimberry, who had risen from clerk to senior vice-president by the time he was 30. His thefts began after he borrowed to buy into a nightclub that failed, and at first he stole only small amounts to buy stock.

Some of his methods were similar to those used by Ted Wolfram, but for the most part, they were simple forgeries. In a *Wall Street Journal* article by John Curley (February 7, 1985), Brimberry was quoted as saying, "It's so easy a 5-year-old could do it."

Brimberry made false entries in at least ten customer accounts that he controlled and created accounts under a variety of names, including his wife's maiden name and those of other relatives and friends. And when an auditor was due to visit (he knew in advance of the visits), he would simply send his wife to a stationery store in downtown St. Louis to purchase blank stock certificates, and he would have a printer in a nearby town print the names of corporations on the certificates. He and his wife signed the phony certificates, almost all of which were made out in the names of obscure companies.

After each audit—in 1977, 1978, and 1980—Brimberry took the phony certificates home and ran them through a shredder in his garage.

With the $16 million that Brimberry and his accomplices stole from Stix, Brimberry bought controlling interest in Stix (for $1 million), using an attorney as a front man. The attorney, James Massa, later became a director and used his position to become a consultant to the firm—at $200 an hour—and promoted Brimberry to senior vice-president. Brimberry also invested heavily in the stock of a number of legitimate companies.

"But he dissipated most of his profits on fast living," Curley's *Wall Street Journal* story reported. "He sank more than $1 million into a Granite City, Ill., mansion with three swimming pools, nearly $100,000 in oak kitchen cabinets and a basement spa. Another house near Phoenix, Ariz., cost $485,000. He chartered private jets for weekend trips to Nassau, Disney World and Las Vegas. He sent his wife on expensive European shopping trips.

"Las Vegas became a twice-monthly haunt. Dogged by guilt and the fear of discovery, Mr. Brimberry says he gambled compulsively, once dropping $150,000 in just 20 minutes. He stayed in posh penthouse suites and treated friends and family to caviar, fine wines, and $400-a-night prostitutes."

SIPC advanced $27.7 million in the Stix case and later recovered $4.8 million of that. Brimberry was sentenced to 10 years for obstruction of justice and another 10 years for perjury and concealing assets. His front man, Massa, got a 20-year sentence. Four other accomplices received lesser sentences.

Gary Lewellyn, responsible for the demise of G. V. Lewellyn & Co., Inc. in Des Moines in April 1982, was the son of a banker. His fraud also caused the collapse of a regional bank in Iowa, the First National Bank of Humboldt, where his father, Clifford Lewellyn, was president.

Lewellyn, 33 at the time, served as the bank's investment broker but often did not actually fill the orders. He simply "bucketed" the orders and sent phony confirmations that the securities were held in safekeeping for his father's bank. He ultimately took more than $16 million from the Humboldt bank (which later reopened as the Hawkeye Bank & Trust Co.) and nearly $2 million from University Trust & Savings Bank of Ames, Iowa.

Lewellyn used much of the money to buy controlling interest in Safeguard Scientifics, Inc., a manufacturer of automotive and machine parts in King of Prussia, Pennsylvania. His attempt to corner the market in the stock led to his undoing. The stock's price fell, Lewellyn's margin debt was called, and as a result he was unable to pay. He left $22 million in unpaid brokerage debts at five firms from which he bought the stock.

Lewellyn had expensive tastes. He owned five high-priced automobiles at one point. He also was a compulsive gambler (in fact, he tried unsuccessfully to present evidence of a "compulsive gambling syndrome" during his trial).

After his fraud was exposed, Lewellyn became a fugitive for three weeks. He abandoned his wife and two children and fled to Las Vegas with a $600,000 bankroll, half of which he gambled away and spent on cars—in that three-week period, he bought a Porsche and a $40,000 Rolls-Royce. He surrendered after talking to a family friend, former Iowa governor and senator Harold Hughes.

The ultimate loss was $17.7 million, most of which the FDIC paid. SIPC paid out more than $1 million. In November 1982 Lewellyn was sentenced to 20 years in prison.

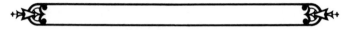

The case of Ted Wolfram and Bell & Beckwith offers the greatest number of lessons for regulators and brokerages because he perpetrated his fraud over a long period of time and used a more elaborate and sophisticated scheme than most white-collar criminals.

Wolfram's fraud worked primarily because he maneuvered himself into a position where he could defeat the normal checks and balances system of a brokerage.

Wolfram was a man with a powerful ego and the kind of ambition that only a man out to impress a woman exhibits. Even the hotel in Las Vegas, from which his wife could operate her own show-production company, was bought mainly as an ego salve.

He first stole to help hide a deficiency in another partner's account just before an audit. Finding out how easily the paperwork could be manipulated, he later began inflating collateral in margin accounts under a variety of names and borrowing against the inflated values to siphon off millions of dollars for his outside business ventures.

In a manner of speaking, Ted Wolfram wrote himself a $47 million bad check. When the Landmark Hotel failed to make money, his thefts became more regular and more desperate. In addition to losing $15 million on the hotel in five years, he poured millions into other ventures designed to provide a stream of income to pay back the worsening hotel debt. Before he was caught, Wolfram had diverted Bell & Beckwith money into a horse farm, several oil and energy companies, ranch land, and cattle.

Wolfram's thefts, covering nearly a decade, also depended on his powers of persuasion. He successfully kept the firm's other partners from questioning his business ventures and his life-style, and he disarmed a series of auditors and examiners by his seeming honesty and integrity.

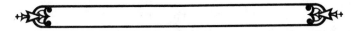

Some of the lessons to be learned from the Bell & Beckwith mess are so rudimentary that they hardly need stating: Don't sign anything you don't understand; don't totally trust a partner whose mistakes you could be liable for; don't give one person sole control of every critical function of a business.

Others are a little less general than that. One Toledo wag, in jest, made a serious point: "Never trust a broker with peacocks on his lawn." Wolfram's peacocks, the gift of a wealthy investor, by themselves probably wouldn't have caused any great suspicions. His 17 personal vehicles, by themselves, might not have created suspicions about extravagance (after all, some of them were part of a collection). Even his three airplanes—given the fact that he owned a hotel in Las Vegas—might not have been a tip-off that he had overextended himself. By all accounts, his various enterprises were doing well. But a reasonable person might ask: How much is too much?

One lesson evidently was learned by thousands of Toledoans whose funds were tied up temporarily in the Bell & Beckwith closing. Brokers reported a dramatic rise in the number of people asking for physical delivery of stock certificates, and some brokerages saw hundreds of customers take possession of certificates that previously had been held in "street name."

(Ironically, that lesson was not learned by the city of Toledo's own treasury department. In 1985, when ESM Government Securities went out of business in Fort Lauderdale, Florida, Toledo was one of numerous cities and institutions that lost more than $300 million. Toledo alone stands to lose almost all its $19 million investment in ESM's repurchase agreements because the city didn't insist on physical delivery of the collateral. One offshoot of that case, reminiscent in some respects of Bell & Beckwith, is that the court-appointed receiver filed a $315 million damage suit against the auditor, Alexander Grant & Co. Other offshoots of the ESM case included a savings and loan holiday for state-insured institutions called by Ohio Governor Richard Celeste and the resignations of Toledo's city manager, treasurer, and finance director.)

There were many other lessons learned from the Bell & Beckwith case. Here's a sampling of the comments from former Bell & Beckwith employees and others who observed the failure firsthand:

• Judge Nicholas Walinski sees the Wolfram fraud, reduced to its simplest element, as a case of "a guy who stole a paper clip and found out he could get away with it. Then, he stole ten paper clips" and eventually 40 million paper clips. "I've always told my children, 'Don't steal that first paper clip,' " Walinski said. An official with the SEC had a similar comment about Wolfram: "He was basically a decent sort of guy who just got in too deep."

• A former broker with Bell & Beckwith who now manages another brokerage: "Things that are supposed to be a protection really weren't a protection. . . . You pay a lot of money to rely on audits, and they didn't catch it." After the demise of Bell & Beckwith, Stix, and now ESM Government Securities, the pressure is on accounting firms to demonstrate their professionalism, but at the same time, investors will have good reason to look beyond the auditing statement when choosing a firm to do business with. Ed Esgain, who had retired as a general partner years before the demise of the firm but whose finances were nevertheless devastated by the collapse, made pretty much the same point a few months before his death. Holding a copy of the 1981 financial-condition report, Esgain said, "I kept getting beautiful statements."

• Barry Sucher, also a former Bell & Beckwith broker now managing a branch office for a Cleveland brokerage, suggests several rules: "Never be a partner in a partnership [one large Ohio brokerage, McDonald & Co., in fact, went public at least partly because of the risk factors made clear in the Bell & Beckwith failure]; ask for full disclosure; outlaw such practices as offering 'special' commission rates to brokers who sell certain stocks [one of Wolfram's tactics in the final months of the firm was to promote a few favorite stocks on which he hoped to make a killing]." And finally: "Someday we're going to stop tempting a broker when he's having a bad month." Sucher feels the opportunity to make a fast commission can cloud the judgment of brokers and make them less observant of possible rules infractions.

• Ted Focht, president of the Securities Investor Protection Corp.: "Who should learn from this? Partners and principals of brokerages, accountants and public auditors, and self-regulatory agencies." Focht has made a number of speeches using the Stix & Co., Lewellyn, and Bell & Beckwith cases as examples of what can go wrong in the system.

He points out that SIPC has no regulatory powers and has a staff of only 36, compared with more than 4,000 on the staff of the Federal Deposit Insurance Corp. He also points out that, in at least a couple of those cases, close relatives and partners of the ones responsible for the fraud were duped until the end.

"Why didn't some of these people ask questions?" he asks. Focht offers recommendations. The industry must be especially alert for fraud by principals and insiders, he said (shortly after the Bell & Beckwith failure, the New

York Stock Exchange pulled a surprise audit of a substantial number of small and medium-size regional firms, looking specifically for accounts of principals and their families). Counterfeit securities played an important role in some of the spectacular failures and should be a target for examiners.

And finally, "Look for excessive concentration. In Bell & Beckwith's last audited statement, it showed 97 percent of the firm's assets were receivables from customers—and a substantial percentage of that was in accounts controlled by insiders."

• A partner in William C. Roney, a regional brokerage based in Detroit: "Bell & Beckwith was too small to have sufficient internal controls. There weren't enough people for all the hats involved." As a minimum, no one person should be in charge of all critical functions in a firm.

The stock-brokerage auditing subcommittee of the American Institute of Certified Public Accountants offers some suggestions in its guide for audits of brokers and dealers in securities: "Margin records should be reviewed periodically by an employee who has no duties in connection with them to determine that the minimum margin requirements of the firm are being maintained. The margin department of a broker or dealer should have a system to prevent violations of Regulation T and similar regulations dealing with the extension and maintenance of credit. Procedures should be in effect to see that all necessary margin calls are made and followed up."

And "separate identification should be maintained for the accounts of all partners, officers, employees, and their known relatives so that transactions in such accounts can be reviewed by an appropriate employee."

• George Mann, Cleveland district director for the National Association of Securities Dealers: "Now we're looking closer at management and how much control they have over the back office. . . . Make damn sure you do an independent evaluation of collateral. Make sure you look at 'em and feel 'em." Mann also says it should be standard practice for a brokerage to double-check margin accounts, looking especially for names similar to those of employees.

• The doctor in Columbus, Indiana, who once employed Zula Wolfram and who lost many thousands of dollars in the collapse: "Paper alone won't do it . . . trust is not enough." He had bought cattle with Wolfram but lacked evidence adequate to recover his investment. Wolfram periodically sent him profit-and-loss statements for tax purposes, but the doctor was not able to convince the trustee that he was a bona fide "investor" in Bell & Beckwith. The doctor, who had once lent Ted and Zula the down payment for a house, blames himself for trusting too much. ". . . I grieve for them [the Wolframs] and for myself."

12

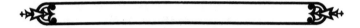

No End in Sight

On the twenty-first day of the twenty-fifth month of the Bell & Beckwith case, U.S. Bankruptcy Court Judge Richard Speer had had about all he could take of an attorney who was monopolizing the discussion on a motion in one of the case's seemingly endless hearings.

With a wave, the judge stopped the lawyer in midsentence and said: "I did not want to make this motion my life's work. I did not want to make this case my life's work, either, but apparently I was mistaken in that notion."

At another point in the hearing—to hear objections to the out-of-court settlement with Arthur Young for $388,000—the judge, a severe-looking man with an acerbic sense of humor, interrupted an overly dramatic argument by saying: "This isn't television. This isn't *Gone with the Wind*. This is just little old me, and I just want to hear some facts."

And in another of the many hearings in the bankruptcy side of the case, Judge Speer, learning of a compromise that would bring the Landmark Hotel and Casino closer to a sale, remarked: "I feel with the effort that's gone into making this compromise, signing it in a rail car somewhere in France would be appropriate."

Judge Speer's bits of levity stood in contrast to the general seriousness of the pursuit of settlements in what remains the case of 1,000 days, even if most of the 7,000 nightmares are over. And, indeed, there is no apparent end in sight.

Even as the statute of limitations approached, these actions were filed:

• A suit against the eight general partners and five former general partners (Richard Foote, Robert Fox, Jr., Louis Haubner, Grafton Mouen, and James Secor, Jr.) for the full amount of the deficiency, whatever it ultimately happens to be. (The suit also alleged that one of the partners, Jesionowski, and his wife, Marilyn, illegally transferred property to her name to keep it out of the trustee's hands.)

• Suits against two Wolfram companies—TZ Explorations and TZ Land and Cattle—for a total of $11 million.

• A suit against Philip J. M. Roth—Wolfram's friend and fellow sports bettor and next-door business neighbor on Erie Street—for $74,606 for recovery of funds withdrawn from a customer account that ended up with a negative net worth.

Many of the trustee's suits for recovery of hundreds of thousands of dollars worth of loans Wolfram made to friends and business acquaintances have been resolved, and many have not. Among those settling up with the trustee were Mark Miller, the former pro football player befriended by Wolfram, who owed $53,674 because of a debit balance in his Bell & Beckwith account.

But many of the actions (such as those seeking settlements from Wolfram's farm land in Missouri and Arkansas, his horse farm in Florida, and his partial ownership of an oil company) went into their third year of litigation—and give every indication of going well beyond that.

The last of the Wolfram family's personal goods have been sold, and some of them brought disappointing amounts of money considering the original cost. House, cars, planes, Las Vegas condo, jewelry, collectibles, paintings—all told brought less than $1 million. In two years, the unusual home never drew an offer close to the $309,000 asking price (it was finally sold at auction for $180,000). One exquisite wildlife painting that was said to be worth as much as $30,000 brought barely a tenth that amount. Wolfram's 17 vehicles—including three Mercedes, two BMWs, a Lamborghini, a Maserati, and eight rare Italian OSCA sports cars—brought less than $250,000 total (Wolfram had valued the OSCA cars at $100,000 apiece, but the highest bid was $31,500).

A testament to the complexity of the Bell & Beckwith and Wolfram cases was the 1,045-page report filed with the bankruptcy court in December 1984. It took 21 months to compile the list of assets and customers' accounts. The massive document contained such information as the fact that there was only $52.17 in cash at Bell & Beckwith's main office at the end of its last day in business, and that the firm's insurance covered only $700,000 of the huge losses. It included a detailed inventory of Wolfram's 455 bottles of wine. The report accounted for $109 million in liabilities and $69 million in assets, leaving a shortage of $40 million.

Here are some of the winners and losers in the tangled and virtually endless Bell & Beckwith case:

WINNERS

• The lawyers. Going into the third year of the case, the legal bills submitted to the bankruptcy court topped the $3 million mark (about $2 million of which was paid in increments over the first two years). Much of the money went to the law firm of Fuller & Henry, the firm that the trustee, Patrick McGraw, was a partner in at the outset of the case. Judge Speer was critical of the legal fees on a number of occasions. At one point, he told trustee McGraw, "You need not have a craftsman doing an apprentice's job." Speer objected to lawyers, paid as much as $115 an hour, carrying out tasks that could have been accomplished by lower-paid staff.

• The accounting firm of Ernst & Whinney, which at times had 20 professionals working on the books of Bell & Beckwith. By the end of the second year of the project, accounting fees and expenses totaled $2.7 million.

• William Morris, who bought the Landmark Hotel and Casino in a deal valued at nearly $20 million. Morris, an experienced casino operator, paid only about $4.2 million in cash and only about $2.5 million at the time of closing. Within a year after he bought the Landmark, he had put several million dollars into renovation of one wing, a new entranceway, new gaming machines, new fireproofing system, new furnishings, and a badly needed renovation of many of the sleeping rooms. Occupancy rates went over 90 percent, and Morris rolled out plans for another high-rise tower on the 21-acre site. Even so, Morris missed the April 1985 deadline for the final payment of $1.7 million to the trustee, who threatened foreclosure action.

• Patrick McGraw, the liquidation trustee. While still trustee for the case, McGraw left his law firm, Fuller & Henry (amid local speculation that his political work for the likes of Walter Mondale had irritated his partners). His experience with the Bell & Beckwith case was the highlight of his career and now fills almost his entire résumé.

• Ralph Buie, the SEC examiner who blew the whistle on Ted Wolfram. Partly because of his efforts in the

Bell & Beckwith case, Buie has been promoted to a staff attorney's position in Atlanta.

• Some private insurance companies. Partly as a result of the Bell & Beckwith, Stix, and Lewellyn cases and the resultant loss in investor confidence, many brokerage firms now offer private insurance that goes beyond SIPC coverage—up to $2.5 million per account in some cases.

LOSERS

• The Securities Investor Protection Corp. (SIPC), which advanced more than $42 million to pay investors of the failed firm. SIPC got back about $3 million of its advances in the first distribution of funds in the bankruptcy, and it stands to get some more money back, depending on the outcome of several important court cases, but it is unlikely that SIPC will recover anywhere near the $39 million left. Brokers and investors all over the country are indirectly helping to pay for the losses, since SIPC imposed an assessment that will remain until its reserves reach $300 million.

• Liberty Airlines, a small regional outfit that was attempting to go public when the brokerage failed. Bell & Beckwith was managing the $2 million offering, but only about $1 million had been transferred to Liberty. The airline was unable to buy equipment it needed to stay in business, and it later was sold at a loss.

• Charles and Mary McKenny, who, along with their family and a family foundation, had about $8 million invested in Bell & Beckwith and millions more invested in partnerships with Ted Wolfram (including some "handshake" deals). The McKennys got all of it back except $879,000 of his money and $858,000 of hers. However, the

McKennys are involved in a number of legal hassles with the trustee—disputes over the value of property jointly owned with Wolfram and a suit against Charles McKenny for $70,000 for securities transactions in his customer account just before the brokerage folded.

• Nine other individuals and two corporations with Bell & Beckwith investments substantially in excess of SIPC insurance limits. They (and the amounts still owed to them) are: Joseph V. Wilson, of Clyde, Ohio, $156,406; John R. Koch, of Orchard Lake, Michigan, $87,079; Dr. Fredrick W. Hiss, of Toledo, $73,595; estate of Joseph J. Schedel, of Elmore, Ohio, $57,825; James F. Thompson, of Vail, Colorado, $59,894; Julie T. Berlacher, of Alexandria, Virginia, $56,095; John E. Thompson, Jr., of Brooklyn, $54,710 (the Thompson brothers and Mrs. Berlacher are the children of John Thompson, one of Bell & Beckwith's general partners); Milton H. Penney, of Vero Beach, Florida, $35,205; Robert E. Hylant, of Toledo, $13,000; Defiance Stamping Co., of Defiance, Ohio, $23,936; and Perfection Finishers, Inc., of Wauseon, Ohio, $2,623.

• The auditors. Arthur Young has already paid $388,000 to avoid litigation over its role as an auditor early in the Wolfram fraud. The case against Frederick S. Todman & Co. for $65 million won't go to trial until three years after the Bell & Beckwith collapse, at the earliest. But the Todman firm already has been censured by the SEC for its practices while auditing Bell & Beckwith in the six years before the collapse.

• The partners. The seven general partners are each fully liable for the amount of the loss under Ohio's partnership laws. Barring an unexpected large recovery of money, the partners face financial ruin. One is already bankrupt. All have been prohibited from owning or managing brokerage firms or investment companies in the future.

• Five former general partners, who face an uncertain liability, depending on how several court cases evolve. Some had been away from Bell & Beckwith for years, but because they signed reports that later turned out to be falsified by Wolfram, they were included in the suits.

• The limited partners. Four of them have lost their investment in Bell & Beckwith, some of which was to have been their retirement income. Ted Wolfram's father, Edward Wolfram, Sr., one of the limited partners, lost $87,540 in his capital account, plus more than $20,000 in drawing accounts and a pension plan. Richard Foote, of Gainesville, Florida, lost $33,024 capital, plus $24,132 in a drawing account. Edward Esgain had $28,074 in a capital account and $18,390 in a drawing account, and he was receiving a $500-a-month pension from Bell & Beckwith. Esgain died in 1985.

• Irene Smith, the fourth limited partner. Mrs. Smith, widow of a former general partner, was one of the objectors to the Arthur Young out-of-court settlement for $388,000. Here's part of the objection:

> Irene Smith is an elderly woman whose late husband was a Bell & Beckwith partner. Following Mr. Smith's death in 1968, the remaining Bell & Beckwith partners invited Mrs. Smith to become a limited partner. She agreed, and her late husband's capital was left with the firm. In February 1983 all of Mrs. Smith's assets (aside from her personal effects in her apartment) were at Bell & Beckwith. She had $130,000 in her capital account and approximately $99,000 on deposit in a draw or regular account. Thus she is a creditor as well as a limited partner. Following the discovery that Edward Wolfram had looted partnership assets, Mrs. Smith has been trying to subsist on her only source of income, her Social Security check, a sum insufficient even to meet the rent on her apartment.

• The Wolfram family. Wolfram's children, parents, and in-laws have been sued for $440,000, plus interest, that the trustee says is owed to the firm, and the trustee sued

Zula Wolfram for $28 million for the deficiencies in her accounts at the time of the failure. (Mrs. Wolfram, in a counterclaim, asked for the return of all the property she signed over to the trustee and $24 million in damages.)

There was another kind of toll on the Wolfram family. An affidavit filed by Zula Wolfram tells one side of that story:

> Prior to February 5, 1983, I had always assumed that my husband, Edward P. Wolfram, Jr., was a very successful investor and businessman. Although some substantial purchases had been made prior to February 5, 1983, Mr. Wolfram frequently assured me that sufficient funds were available. . . . I believed that all assets acquired by my husband and I were acquired with funds that were obtained lawfully.
>
> On February 5, 1983, my husband called our entire family together for a meeting. At that meeting he announced that for a period of time he had been stealing money from Bell & Beckwith. Prior to that announcement neither I nor any of the members of my family had knowledge of his wrongdoing.
>
> . . . Prior to that date we had enjoyed the respect of our community and had a good reputation. The announcement of the fraud, together with the extraordinary press coverage and convergence on our house of numerous lawyers from Bell & Beckwith created a state of turmoil and upheaval in my family and in my life. For a substantial period of time following the announcement I was in a state of shock and confusion.

Mrs. Wolfram's statement went on to say that her husband's attorneys told her she had no choice but to sign over her property because her assets would be taken anyway and that she received no independent legal advice.

> Between the discovery of my husband's fraud and his incarceration, I did not have the time to obtain an attorney or otherwise to cancel or rescind the assignments. During this period, all of my time was directed to holding myself and my family together. My husband's emotional state had deteriorated

substantially and I at times feared for his physical health. The revelation of the fraud also affected my children, one of whom was still in high school. It was not until approximately October 3, 1983, when my husband began serving his sentence that I had time to think about the events of the past eight months and their effect on me.

One of the Wolframs' daughters, Paula Jean Nemeth, filed an affidavit at the same time that gave more details of the effect of the collapse on the Wolfram family:

. . . At approximately 7:00 A.M. on February 5, 1983, I received a phone call from my father. My father told me to get dressed and to come over to my parents' home [from McClure, Ohio] because he wanted to talk to me. When I arrived at the house with my husband and son I saw that my father had also called my other brothers and sisters. Edward P. Wolfram III (Fritz) and his wife and three children were present. My brother Ian was also there. My sister Roxanne [Ziss] and her husband were living in Maine and were unable to attend. When Frank J. P. McManus [the family attorney] arrived, my father made an announcement.

My father announced to us that he was a thief and that for a period of time had systematically stolen $40,000,000 from Bell & Beckwith. He also announced that he was going to jail and that life as we had known it was coming to an end. My father's discussion lasted for approximately five minutes. I was seated next to my mother during his discussion and observed her both during my father's talk and after. Immediately after the talk ended my mother turned white and began to shake. From that moment on, and for a substantial number of months following the announcement, my mother acted like a zombie. She would lose her train of thought and be unable to complete tasks she was engaged in.

On February 5, my mother also became very frightened. She was told that my father would go to jail. She was also told that because her name was on various accounts she could be prosecuted even though she was not involved in any of the wrongdoing. We also began receiving numerous phone calls from irate customers and Bell & Beckwith partners. Those phone calls began in the evening of February 5 [after the court hearing that closed the brokerage down]. My mother became very concerned that an irate customer might become violent and she asked my husband to patrol the grounds at night. Specifically, she was afraid that someone might set her house on fire.

On the morning of February 6, I heard my mother phone my brother Fritz and ask him to come to the house. When he arrived she asked him to remove my father's shotgun from the house. My mother told us that she was afraid my father would commit suicide.

On February 5th and 6th, my mother told me that she was afraid that my father's actions were going to cause her children to lose everything they had.

. . . On both February 5th and 6th, my mother appeared to be in a state of shock. On February 6th she was asked to sign several documents at my parents' home. . . . Because of my concern about my mother and father's emotional condition I moved in their home on February 5 and stayed there through February 11, 1983. Throughout that period, and on February 6, 1983, my mother repeatedly told me that she did not know who to go to for advice. She told me that all of the lawyers were dad's lawyers and that all of the people that were supporting the family at that time were dad's friends. She told me that she didn't know what to do and that nobody seemed to care about her or her problems.

Zula Wolfram is now living in Las Vegas, working for Gary Yelverton at Maxim's. Yelverton had helped the Wolframs buy a controlling interest in the Landmark Hotel and Casino, and he later owned a small share of the hotel himself.

And then there's Ted Wolfram himself. Unless there's a change of heart on the part of the parole commissioners, he will go well beyond his sixtieth birthday in prison. Although it was originally supposed he would be paroled after serving 40 to 52 months of his 25-year sentence, the recommendation now is that he serve ten years. His request to withdraw his guilty plea was denied. The

Tallahassee prison is, for the most part, a white-collar criminal facility; it even has tennis courts, a running track, and a miniature golf course. However, there is work to be done, and most of the prisoners labor in a large woodworking factory, making furniture for the armed forces. In his correspondence Wolfram has said that he is writing a book; presumably to tell his side of the Bell & Beckwith story.

Whatever length of time Wolfram actually serves, his thoughts must be many and difficult. No one, not even Wolfram, will know if he could have gotten totally away with his crime if his luck had been better. Perhaps the most difficult thoughts of all could come only to a person who, as an altar boy, dispensed incense and lit the candles of a thousand high masses and read faithfully from his daily missal such prayers of penance as this:

> My Lord and my God, how numerous and manifold are the sins of my past life; how deserving of punishment do I appear before Thy infinite holiness and majesty! . . . Good God, what have I done? I have offended Thee more grievously than many who are now burning in the eternal fire of hell.

Author's Postscript

This saga ends pretty much as it began, with a breaking news story.

Early in March of 1985, more than two years after the Bell & Beckwith disaster, a bulletin came across the news wire about the failure of ESM Government Securities in Fort Lauderdale. The rumor was that the city of Toledo had lost a tremendous amount of money in the collapse of the Florida investment firm.

Surely the rumor couldn't be true. But it was, and so were the shock waves that it created. It was déja vu: Lives were uprooted, long and expensive court battles began, and the repercussions promised to linger just as long as those that attended the Bell & Beckwith scandal. The ESM failure led to Ohio's savings and loan crisis. That crisis in turn led to political charges and countercharges and stoked the worst sort of conjecture. In one week, for example, the savings and loan crisis was blamed for the weakening of the dollar, the drop in consumer confidence, and the sharp rise in the price of gold.

Within weeks, déja vu again: The Toledo branch of Cowen & Co., which had opened just after the Bell & Beckwith fraud became known, closed on short notice. The word circulated over the noon hour on a Thursday, and the office was shut down the next day. Officially, Cowen spokesmen would say only that the office was closed for "economic reasons." But, as the *Blade* said in a news story, the Cowen & Co. branch—staffed mostly by former Bell & Beckwith brokers—had struggled under Bell & Beckwith's shadow over its entire two years in business.

One of the Cowen brokers, also a former Bell & Beckwith employee, is now in his third brokerage job in two and a half years. He lost his sideline business, largely because of the financial pressure brought on by the Bell & Beckwith failure. He also lost a long, costly legal fight with the trustee. And finally he was forced into bankruptcy.

A cloud still hangs over the former Bell & Beckwith partners. For them and for the investment community at large, Bell & Beckwith appears to be the bad penny that keeps coming back.

APPENDIX

How the
Securities Investor
Protection Corp.
Works

(Excerpted from informational pamphlets published by the Securities Investor Protection Corp.)

SIPC protects securities customers of member broker-dealers. If a member fails financially, SIPC may ask a federal court to appoint a trustee to liquidate the firm and protect its customers, or in limited situations involving smaller firms, SIPC may protect the customers directly. In both cases, protection of securities customers is similar.

The trustee and SIPC may arrange to have some or all customer accounts transferred to another SIPC member broker-dealer. Customers whose accounts are transferred are notified promptly and permitted to deal with the new firm or subsequently transfer their accounts to firms of their own choosing. Accounts so transferred are subject to the limitations of protection discussed below. This procedure minimizes disruption in customers' trading activities. In many cases (for example, where failed firms' records are inaccurate), account transfers are not feasible. SIPC then protects customers' accounts in the following manner:

• Customers of a failed firm receive all securities registered in their names or in the process of being so registered and which are not by endorsement or otherwise in negotiable form.

• Customers receive, on a pro rata basis, all remaining customer cash and securities held by the firm.

• After the above distribution, SIPC's funds are available to satisfy the remaining claims of each customer up to a maximum of $500,000, including up to $100,000 on claims for cash (as distinct from claims for securities). . . .

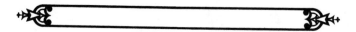

"Customers" are persons with claims for securities received, acquired or held by the firm from or for the securities accounts of such persons for safekeeping, with a view to sale, to cover consummated sales, pursuant to purchases, as collateral security or for purposes of effecting a transfer. Persons who have cash on deposit with a firm for the purpose of purchasing securities or as a result of sales thereof are also considered "customers."

Cash on deposit with a SIPC member for the purpose of earning interest or for any purpose other than purchasing securites is neither included within a customer's "net equity" nor protected under the Act.

A person is not considered a "customer" under the Act to the extent that his claim (a) is for cash or securities which, by contract, agreement, or understanding, or by operation of law, is part of the capital of the firm or is subordinated to the claims of creditors of the firm, or (b) arises out of transactions with a foreign subsidiary of the firm. . . .

Most types of securities, such as notes, stocks, bonds and certificates of deposit, are covered. No protection, however, is provided for unregistered investment contracts or for any interest in gold, silver or other commodity, or commodity contract, or commodity option.

Cash balances are protected under the Securities Investor Protection Act if the money was deposited or left in a securities account for the purpose of purchasing securities. This is true whether or not the broker pays interest on the cash balances. Of course, cash balances maintained solely for the purpose of earning interest are not protected.

SIPC presumes that cash balances are left in securities accounts for the purpose of purchasing securities. It would require substantial evidence to the contrary to overcome the presumption. Standing alone, the fact that a cash balance was earning interest and was not used to purchase securities for a considerable period of time, say several months, would not be sufficient to overcome the presumption.

As a general rule, most customers can expect to receive their property in one to three months. When the records of the firm are accurate, deliveries of some securities and cash to customers may begin shortly after the trustee receives the completed claim forms from customers, or even earlier if the trustee can transfer customer accounts to another broker-dealer. On the other hand, there may be delays of several months where the firm's records are not accurate, or where it appears that the firm or its principals were involved in fraudulent activities. Some delays also may be caused by the need to send stock certificates to transfer agents with specific instructions to issue smaller denominations and issue certificates in other names. This can be a time-consuming operation.

All exchange-traded securities option positions will be closed with the exception of covered short positions when the customer's broker has caused the cover to be deposited with either its correspondent broker or the Options Clearing Corporation. The fact that the customer has given his broker the underlying securities does not guarantee the position is covered for purposes of a SIPC liquidation proceeding; accordingly, a customer with a short option position should ascertain whether cover has been so deposited.

SIPC's funds may not be used to pay claims of any customer who also is: (1) a general partner, officer, or director of the firm; (2) the benficial owner of five per cent or more of any class of equity security of the firm (other than certain nonconvertible preferred stocks); (3) a limited partner with a participation of five per cent or more in the net assets or net profits of the firm; (4) someone with the power to exercise a controlling influence over the management or policies of the firm; or (5) a broker or dealer or bank acting for itself rather than for its own customer or customers.

The money required to protect customers beyond that which is available from the property in the possession of the failed broker-dealer is advanced by SIPC from a fund maintained for that purpose. The sources of money for the SIPC Fund are assessments collected from SIPC members and interest on investments in United States Government securities.

In an emergency, SIPC may borrow up to $1 billion from the U.S. Treasury through the Securities and Exchange Commission if the Commission determines such a loan is necessary to protect customers and maintain confidence in United States securities markets. SIPC must present a plan which provides as reasonable an assurance of prompt repayment as may be feasible under the circumstances. If the Commission determines industry assessments would not satisfactorily repay the loan, it may impose a transaction fee on purchasers of equity securities at a rate not exceeding $\frac{1}{50}$ of 1% of the purchase price ($.20 per $1,000). This fee would not apply to transactions of less than $5,000.

Index